JOHN TEMPLE'S

Asian Insight

(From the television series co-produced with the Australian Broadcasting Commission and Film Australia)

University of Queensland Press

©University of Queensland Press
St. Lucia, Queensland, 1977

Typeset, printed and bound by Academy Press Pty. Ltd.,
Brisbane.

Distributed in the United Kingdom, Europe, the Middle
East, Africa, and the Caribbean by Prentice-Hall
International, International Book Distributors Ltd.,
66 Wood Lane End, Hemel Hempstead, Herts., England

National Library of Australia
Cataloguing-in-publication data

Temple, John, 1930–.
    Asian insight.

    Index.
    Bibliography.
    ISBN   0 7022 1088 9.

    1. Asia—Civilization. I. Title. (Series).

950

For Avril

Contents

Illustrations

THAILAND

Introduction

The intention of the televison series *Asian Insight*, on which this book is based, was to introduce audiences to the cultures and histories of a selection of Asian societies. That seemed to be a useful and interesting thing to do. The questions were where to do it and how to do it.

We (that is Arch Nicholson, the film director, and I) decided to exclude immediately any countries which seemed likely to impose too many restrictions on filming. This was not a current affairs series and we did not plan to go in hard-nosed, prying and exposing, but we did need the freedom to pursue our storylines wherever they led. In the event we were allowed to do this everywhere.

We decided finally on our seven subjects because they formed a reasonably close geographical group whose histories interlocked through population movement, colonialism, conquest, trade and cultural influence. At the same time they offered sufficient contrast to save the films from repetition, visually and otherwise.

We tried not to peep out at the Asian societies through a curtain of our own, Western, culture, or to make too many judgments based on a value system foreign, indeed irrelevant, to the people whose guests we were.

Asian Insight on the screen was really a series of television essays, although it did not occur to us to use that word at the time. It was clearly impossible to offer a definitive account of any society in fifty minutes. Decisions on what to talk about were based simply on what seemed to me to be interesting, and to be relevant to an explanation of how the societies had become what they are.

I have expanded the scripts here and there, sometimes adding detail for which we could find no room in the films. Several passages which depended on a certain kind of film montage have been rewritten to suit the printed page.

From the beginning of the project I have depended on the help and encouragement, as well as the sharp professional eye, of Arch Nicholson. Over the two years which it took to research, shoot, and edit the series we both leaned heavily on the unflagging energy and skill of Damien Parer, unit manager; Dean Semler and Andrew Fraser, cameramen; Peter Lipscomb, sound recordist; and Peter Vile, film editor.

I am eager to acknowledge my indebtedness to many sources of scholarship and local expertise. To some extent I have recorded this in the select bibliography—a list which may seem rather idiosyncratic, but which is as accurate a tally as I can make of books which in varying degrees provided facts, argument, hypotheses, and local colour. To fit the available time and to allow the narrative to flow I have occasionally made an arbitrary, but I hope not frivolous, choice from among conflicting scholarly views. Such flowers of learning as appear in the book are other men's. The weeds are mine.

It is a pleasure to acknowledge my gratitude to: Professor S.H. Alatas, Zain Arif, Mr. and Mrs. Stan Barney, Michiko Blair, Father Horacio de la Costa, the Rev. Dr. Hiraoka, Richard Hughes, Victor Kennedy, Father Joseph Love, Mr. and Mrs. John Milne, Peter Ngeow, Mr. and Mrs. Brian Peck, Jaime Picornell, Mr. and Mrs. Neil Smail, Brigid Snow, Dhira Soehoed, Mr. and Mrs. Gabino Tabunar Jr., Professor Emannuel Torres, and Mr. and Mrs. Bob Wollbrink.

With a few exceptions which are acknowledged separately, all the illustrations in the book are from colour negative stills shot by Peter Lipscomb. I very much admire his skill with the camera, and gladly record my gratitude for it.

John Temple

1 Japan

The Bamboo Bends and Does Not Break

Modern Japan is a visually exciting mixture of gleaming technology, raucous commercialism, and traditional ways of thought and behaviour. All Asian societies show these contrasts and tensions, but Japan alone has made the tensions dynamic, producing enormous social energy, stability, and a capacity to absorb change.

Everyone knows Japan is a paradox. The "bullet train" from Osaka to Tokyo skims at 200 k.p.h. over rice fields which still use irrigation techniques the Japanese have known for more than a thousand years. It passes Mount Fuji, sacred to the ancient Shinto cult, and factories producing marvels of micro-electronics. Arriving in Tokyo, its passengers may head for a school teaching the subtle harmonies of *ikebana* flower arrangement, or for a nightclub where it is not unusual for a bottom-pinching businessman to spend $500 on a one-night binge.

1. *Ikebana*, the art of flower arrangement first used as a discipline by Buddhist monks. An *ikebana* teacher has said the aim is to establish "peace and harmony between the flowers, and between the flowers and the surroundings, and between the flower's heart and my heart".

2. The "bullet train" passing Mount Fuji. (Photograph by courtesy of the Japanese National Tourist Organization.)

Western writers have been struggling to understand Japanese society ever since it opened its doors to the West a little more than a hundred years ago. The Japanese are polite, and arrogant; they are docile, and aggressive; they are sensitive and kind, but also unfeeling and sometimes even brutal. The contradictions are seemingly endless. Surely they cannot all be true?

Two things can be said about that. Firstly, all these judgments about Japan are made from within a Western system of values. To a Japanese, many of the apparent contradictions are not in conflict at all. Secondly, there are two threads which intertwine through the whole of Japanese history, and help to resolve the paradox. One is the concept of loyalty, duty, and obligation. The other is the powerful sense of group, of "us" and "them". These threads have held together the vertical structure of Japanese society so that in its parts it is rigid, but as a whole, supple. To unravel these threads is to begin to understand what it is that makes Japan so Japanese.

Their culture began at Mount Miwa, near Nara in central Japan. The story of Mount Miwa is bound up in the myths which gather about the early history of all peoples. At about the time of the beginning of the Christian era in Europe, mongoloid people invaded Japan through Korea and organized themselves into clans. One of the clans lived around Mount Miwa. To them, the mountain was both a god itself, and the dwelling place of gods. This was the beginning, in simple animism and nature-worship, of the faith called Shinto.

3. Wet rice cultivation, a technique the Japanese have practised for more than a thousand years.

The grand-daughter of one of the local gods, so the legend goes, became the consort of the leader of another powerful clan, the Yamatos. It is not certain that this leader of the Yamatos was a real historical personage, but that is beside the point. His name was Jimmu. He set up a court at Miwa or thereabouts and came to be regarded, and revered, as the first emperor of Japan.

Stripped of its mythical poetry, the story is a familiar one in early societies. One clan, the Yamatos, who had settled in the south somewhere near Nagasaki, made their way north in the course of a few centuries, and established leadership of all the clan states in the heartland of Japan. The chief of the Yamato clan became the chief of all the clans, and the religious cult of the Yamatos became the cult of the emerging nation. The cult was that of the sun goddess, Amaterasu. Her shrine is still venerated today, at the foot of Mount Miwa, under the twisted rope which marks places sacred to the Shinto cult.

The Emperor Jimmu was held to be a direct descendant of the sun goddess. Only direct descendants, thereafter, could be emperor. The present emperor is the 124th in the line. The tradition established at Mount Miwa became a central tenet of Shinto, and an important part of the Japanese ethos. The first and most important of all loyalties, the one on which all others hang, is that owed to the emperor.

The early Japanese clans were simple farmers, but their leaders, apparently, were men of vision. In 552, Buddhist missionaries arrived from Korea, bringing not only a faith but architects, sculptors, and skilled artisans. The Yamato rulers, sending emissaries to report on the glitter and sophistication of the T'ang court of China, realized the deficiencies of their own society which so far had no written script, nor even a city. They decided to import a civilization, and began the long Japanese history of judicious, selective borrowing.

The first centre of scholarship and of the Buddhist religion was the temple of Horyu-ji, built in 607 by Crown Prince Shotoku. It is still there, on the outskirts of Nara. Its style is Chinese, with infusions of more distant influence such as some Greek architectural principles, which had come to China along the Silk Road. Japan had made itself the heir of several civilizations of great age and subtlety.

The first capital was Nara, built in 710. Today Nara is a messy conglomeration of temples, shrines, industry, and suburbia. It has a population of nearly 300,000, and a million tourists come every year to admire the monuments of a golden age of Buddhist culture.

By the eighth century, enthusiasm for Buddhism had become a craze. Noble families competed to outbuild each other with temples. The Emperor Shomu, who was ruling at the time, could not, of course, be outdone. He decreed that every province should have its

temple, and that he would have the chief of them all. He built the
colossal wooden temple of Todai-ji. It is still the largest wooden structure in the world, although much of it has been destroyed several
times in fires over the centuries, and carefully rebuilt.

The sense of grandeur, of cosmic destiny, which recurred later in
Japanese history first asserted itself in Todai-ji. Earlier, Horyu-ji tem-
ple had been dedicated to Sakyamuni Gautama, the original historical
Buddha. But not Todai-ji. It was built to house a Buddha embodying
the central principle of truth of the whole universe. The Buddha
Vairocana, the cosmic Buddha, the Daibutsu. The Great Buddha.

The first sight of the Buddha, on stepping over the wooden
threshold of the Great Buddha Hall, catches the breath. The original
casting in the middle of the eighth century took five years. The Buddha is nearly twenty-two metres high, including the pedestal. The
Japanese say that twenty men can stand in the palm of its out-
stretched hand. It weighs 560 tonnes. It is Japan's first triumph of
technology. But more than that, the Daibutsu is a symbol of a society
growing in self-confidence.

It was made more than a thousand years after the time of the
historical Buddha. By the time Mahayana Buddhism, or the northern

4. The Daibutsu—the Great
Buddha—of Todai-ji temple,
Nara.

5. Footbridge over a lake in
the gardens of the Heian
Shrine, Kyoto.

school, arrived in Japan it was split into many sects with a bewildering pantheon of deities only vaguely connected with the original Indian faith. The smaller hall of Sangatsu-do in the grounds of Todai-ji is a treasure-house of varied influences. The main figure is Indian in style. An attendant figure is Chinese. The pattern on the robe of a guardian deity is Persian. And emerging in the delicate clay figures of goddesses of sunlight and moonlight is a style which is identifiably Japanese.

Despite its art and scholarship, the court at Nara became priest-ridden and corrupt. In 794 the court moved some kilometres north to Kyoto, and a time of consolidation began. The four centuries from 794 to 1185 became known as the Heian Period. In the nineteenth century the Japanese people built a memorial to this crucial time in their history—the Heian Shrine and garden, in Kyoto.

Already, at the start of the Heian Period, the Japanese were accepting a wide range of cultural equipment—writing, styles of building and painting, even new philosophical and religious concepts—while leaving undisturbed the basic order they thought was right for them. They did not adopt the Chinese system of examination for official appointments, preferring caste and the proper

place to scholarship and social mobility. Without disturbing their loyalty to the emperor, the provincial barons were feeling their power, and extending it at each other's expense. To do this they created a very important class of retainers with sworn loyalty, the warriors.

The tensions were obvious in a society with a supposedly absolute ruler and a squabbling collection of ambitious warlords. Something had to snap, and eventually it did. In the meantime, though, Kyoto produced a remarkable flowering of art and aesthetic appreciation. It was the art of a sensitive and leisured aristocracy, an art of privilege. It used techniques originally learned from China, but its essential qualities by now were Japanese. They sprang from the glittering, hothouse culture of the Kyoto court.

Architecture strove for an appearance of harmony with nature. Gardens were made to emphasize a sense of peace and order. On screens and partitions inside the buildings painters drew out the essence of seasons in the landscape. The early, primitive sense of identification with nature, of worship of mountains, trees, and animals, became intellectualized under the influence of Buddhism. The primitive sense of wonder and awe took on a tinge of melancholy.

The gracefulness and sensuality of the Heian style are almost feminine. The nobles sighing under their painted screens welcomed new Buddhist sects, including the Jodo, or Pure Land, cult which worshipped a mythical Buddha called Amida. By calling on the name of this tender, compassionate Buddha one could hope to be reborn in paradise. The formula was simple. The noble class found it attractive. Devotees built splendid shrines to the Amida Buddha. One nobleman built a pavilion to represent what he hoped paradise would be like when he got there: the Phoenix Hall of Byodo-in temple. Buildings such as the Phoenix Hall used the very latest architectural principles and exquisite craftsmanship. Like all the artistic enterprise of the Heian period they set going a current, a pulse of feeling, which finds a response in Japanese creativity even today.

6. The Phoenix Hall of Byodo-in temple, Kyoto, built by a devotee of the Amida Buddha.

Tokyo architect Kisho Kurokawa:

In European aesthetics, as maybe in ancient Greece or Rome, aesthetics must be based on eternity, art and architecture must have the characteristics of eternity. But in Japan beauty or aesthetics are based on time. Everything must be changed. So maybe if you experience Tokyo it's a sort of disorder, chaos; but for the Japanese Tokyo has order because Tokyo is always changing. In this process of changing we are trying to get continuity between the culture and technology, so we don't have a master plan or final plan. We don't believe in a final plan. Thus we can get a more dynamic process, we can find how we can fit the environment to the contemporary way of life. So I think in architecture or civic planning we prefer the unsymmetrical order. I think it is very similar to traditional

7. The moat of the Imperial Palace, Tokyo.

8. Free-form Japanese architecture—part of the Olympic complex, Tokyo.

Japanese architecture. Symmetry is the confidence of eternity, but Japanese architecture is sometimes very dynamic, very free form. It means the aesthetics of time.

After some four hundred years of consolidation the Heian court had brought into being a truly indigenous culture—but at a price. The court had grown effete. Its tender sensibilities are caught in the scroll painting illustration of the *Tale of Genji*, a novel written at the beginning of the eleventh century by a woman, the Lady Murasaki. It is the first masterpiece of Japanese literature, a tale of courtly love, refined passions, and self-indulgent melancholy. Such elegant preoccupations were shattered at the end of the twelfth century by the beginning of Japan's medieval age, a time of wars.

As times changed so did art. The emperor, whose person was sacred, was left undisturbed in Kyoto, but the real centre of power shifted as first one and then another provincial warlord established supremacy as military dictator, or *shogun*. The next four hundred turbulent years during which Japan moved towards final unity as a nation left deep impressions on the Japanese race memory. It was recalled, for instance, during World War II by the use of a terrible name. Twice in the thirteenth century the Mongol armies of Kublai Khan tried to invade Japan. They failed, because each time most of their ships were lost in typhoons. The Japanese took this as a sign that their land was sacred and inviolable. They called the typhoons Divine Wind. The Japanese for divine wind is *kamikaze*.

The middle ages were not only a time of wars. They were a time of religious expansion also. Buddhism moved out of the court and into ordinary society. Religious art, priestly biographies, and histories of the temples helped spread the Buddhist faith of several new sects, some offering enlightenment in this life, some an escape from the treadmill of reincarnation, some a grisly vision of hell.

Ordinary people began to appear as important figures in narrative painting, not merely as a background for a mincing elite. Farmers, merchants, and more lowly people began to identify themselves as social groups, each with a proper place. The burgeoning Japanese Spirit, as it was later called, began to absorb another influence: the Buddhist teaching called Zen.

Zen Buddhism, brought from China, offered enlightenment through meditation. It required no absolute dependence on sacred formulas, faith in a saviour, or scripture. The enlightenment it sought was an immediate perception of ultimate reality. It made no attempt, and in fact denied the possibility of any attempt, to explain what this reality might be or to understand it intellectually. It was permissible, however, to explore the natural world aesthetically in poetry and painting. The spareness of Zen art sought to suggest the presence of Buddha in everything by a refinement to purity of form. The same suggestive simplicity appeared in Zen gardens. Students of meditation were helped in their concentration by puzzles and paradoxes which, apparently, had no answer. "What", asked a Zen master, "is the sound of one hand?"

Zen taught, and still does, that there are various *do* or Ways which are aids to the discipline needed for enlightenment. They may be peaceful and elegant, like calligraphy and flower arrangement, or martial and elegant, like *judo* and *kendo*, the swordsman's art. They all pursue a Taoist paradox from China: "To see the universal rhythm, find the stillness in movement." All the Ways require great self-discipline and long training in technique. To discover order, harmony, balance without false symmetry, the aim is to transcend technique. "Enter at one stroke," says a Zen master.

9. Corner of a Zen moss garden, Kyoto.

The property which all the Ways have in common (if they are pursued properly) is their difficulty. Their emphasis on training, self-discipline, and commitment to action had a great appeal for the more sophisticated among the warriors of the middle ages. There were the seeds there of a code which was awaiting its time to flower.

The last of the great faiths to enter Japan—and, as it turned out, the least influential—was Christianity. It has an extraordinary and moving early history, beginning at Nagasaki on the southern island of Kyushu. A modern reminder of the story is Oura Roman Catholic church in Nagasaki, built in 1864 by a group of newly arrived missionaries. A few months after it had been built a group of Japanese approached one of the priests. They said they had recognized the cross on top of the church and the statue of the blessed virgin at the entrance. They told the astonished priest that some thousands of people in the Nagasaki area were already Christians and that a Christian community had existed there, secretly and at great risk, for two hundred years.

When Tokyo was still a village in a swamp Nagasaki was Japan's first international city. In the early middle ages boats sailed from its splendid harbour to India and Indonesia, and, according to some scholars, even to Polynesia. Korean and Chinese traders and missionaries entered Japan through Nagasaki. In 1549 direct Western influence arrived with St. Francis Xavier and two other Jesuit missionaries, closely followed by Portuguese and Dutch traders. The traders did well, so well that Portugal founded its colony of Macao, on the China mainland, as a staging post.

St. Francis Xavier left Japan in 1552, having made little headway. Other missionaries stayed and more arrived, both Jesuits and Franciscans, and by the end of the sixteenth century were making fair progress with several hundred thousand converts. Then they had a fatal falling out among themselves. The *shogun* of the time, Hideyoshi, thought that in the dissension between Spanish and Portuguese priests he caught a whiff of local political intrigue. He ordered the expulsion of the missionaries and the destruction of all their work. The ensuing savage campaign to suppress Christianity has turned out to be part of a cyclic pattern in Japanese history—first a welcoming then a fierce rejection of foreign influence.

In Nagasaki in 1597, twenty Japanese converts and six missionaries chose to die rather than deny the faith, and were crucified. The martyrs were canonized in 1862, and are remembered today by a modern church and a memorial. The martyrdom of the twenty-six was followed by events even more terrible. Persecution continued, and in 1637 several thousand Christians on Shimabara peninsula near Nagasaki and on a small island nearby, rose up in arms against it. A

10. The modern church in Nagasaki which commemorates the twenty-six martyrs crucified in 1597 for refusing to deny their Christian faith.

new *shogun* sent warriors against them and put to the sword 30,000 men, women, and children. The Shimabara massacre marked the closing of Japan to the rest of the world for two hundred years. The man who slammed the door was Tokugawa Ieyasu, the first and the greatest of the Tokugawa *shoguns*. Although Ieyasu was not himself responsible for the Shimabara massacre, which was ordered by his grandson, he *was* responsible for the anti-Christian policy which grew, by 1640, into the almost complete exclusion of foreigners. From 1603 to the middle of the nineteenth century *shoguns* of the Tokugawa house kept succeeding emperors immured, luxuriously enough, in the Kyoto court. The *shoguns* always treated the emperors with elaborate courtesy and spoke of them respectfully, but it was the *shoguns* who ruled and bound the nation tight in disciplined unity.

The social values which had been evolving out of Japanese experience since the nation began were refined under the Tokugawas, and formalized. Society was divided into four main groups: *samurai*, farmers, artisans, and merchants—in that order. Above them were the court, the *shoguns* and the *daimyo*, or feudal barons. Below them were miscellaneous groups such as actors, and last of all the outcasts. The cement of the system was loyalty to superiors, whether the emperor, the *shogun*, the *daimyo*, or the father of a family, and loyalty to the group which shared that primary loyalty. The system was closely administered from the capital, Edo, later to be renamed Tokyo or "eastern capital". All provincial barons had to spend every other year in the capital, at their own considerable expense, to keep them out of mischief.

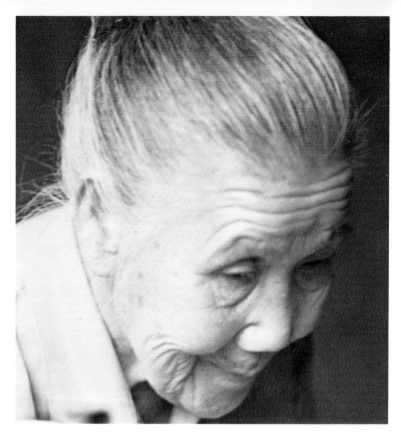

11. An old woman of the outcast Burakumin community.

There are some painful legacies of the Tokugawas' strict division of society, such as the Burakumin, an outcast group whose origins were probably in the fact that they offended against religious taboos by following trades to do with death or the products of dead animals, like leatherwork. They were racially Japanese but were outside the system. They were not "us", they were "them". They were almost non-people, to the extent that the piece of road which passed through their village was not counted in the total mileage. The Burakumin still exist as a group, and are still in a sense outcast today, despite legal assurances of equality. There are probably more than a million Burakumin, some living apparently ordinary lives and fearfully hiding their ancestry, others still living in ghettos in the cities and larger towns. Some Burakumin are highly educated, but if their ancestry is discovered it is difficult for them to hold a good job or to marry into a non-Burakumin family. Ordinary Japanese deny that they believe the old, semi-magical nonsense about the Burakumin being "unclean", but many of them behave as though they believed it.

The Tokugawa period had more general lasting effects on Japanese society. We need to be careful not to interpret these effects merely in terms of arid social discipline.

Father Maurice Bairy, S.J., a psychologist who has lived and taught in Japan for many years:
If we look at the contemporary Japanese society and try to discern what remains from this Tokugawa period we can certainly identify the sense of hierarchy, the sense of loyalty, the sense of discipline. Now these

characteristics can be considered a little too strictly, or too much from a Western point of view. As a matter of fact Japan should be considered as a great organism where all the parts are interdependent and between which there must be a constant exchange of information, of material, of whatever can contribute to the greatest life of the organism and of the various parts of the organism. Now this interdependence necessitates some kind of dependency, and here we touch what the great Japanese psychiatrist Takeo Doi has called *amaeru*—"to be dependent". The Japanese are essentially dependent. All of them are dependent on each other, so that the society should not be considered as a mere arrangement of superiors and inferiors, but as a totality where everybody is biologically linked to the source of life—which is Japan.

Ieyasu, the founder of the Tokugawa house, spent the last few years of his life arranging his own deification and the building of a grandiose shrine in Nikko, in the hills north of Tokyo. The Nikko shrine reflects a cultural change of the Edo period. Artistic styles became more colorful, vigorous, sometimes vulgar. Edo itself developed a lively urban culture. It also developed a notorious "floating world" of popular theatres, brothels, and other places of entertainment.

12. Two boys dressed for the annual historical pageant at the shrine of Tokugawa Ieyasu, Nikko.

The orthodox philosophy of the Tokugawa time was a development of Confucianism: filial piety, stern morality within the hierarchy of obligations, acceptance of one's lot in life. A sense of nationalism grew with isolation. The native cult of Shinto revived. Buddhism began to decline in influence, but not before Confucianism had combined with some aspects of Zen Buddhism and hardened into a code of principle and poetry called Bushido—the Way of the *samurai*. The code embodied Confucian concepts of honour and obligation, and made them rhyme with Buddhist ideas of transience, the frailty of life, the cosmic wheel. Dying was not itself important and may be required, in honour, at any time. To live uprightly was good. To die beautifully was better. The code celebrated the aesthetics of death.

An adherent of the code was expected to commit himself to action in the spirit of the martial arts, and to acquire the discipline and skill of those arts. He was also expected to be a contemplative man, sensitive in spirit, ready to die for his own honour or in pursuit of his obligations. A paragon, indeed.

The code of Bushido romanticized the *samurai* at a time when his heyday as a fighting man was over. The *samurai*'s two swords and distinctive hairstyle mark him out today, in films and television soap operas for the suburban millions. Like Americans with the code of the old West, or Australians with the mateship of the outback, the Japanese luxuriate in nostalgia for the imagined days when men were men. The conflict in *samurai* films, however, has a certain subtlety. With the derring-do there goes, usually, a conflict of obligations to be resolved only in death. The most famous of these stories, retold countless times in books and films, is the *Tale of the Forty-seven Ronin. Ronin* ("wave men") are *samurai* without a lord to serve.

13. Filming a *samurai* soap-opera in a Kyoto studio.

It's a true story. In 1703 a provincial *daimyo* was provoked by an enemy into the terrible offence of drawing his sword in the *shogun*'s palace, and was beheaded. His forty-seven *samurai* disbanded and pretended to have lost their honour and to be living profligate lives. A year later they met secretly, attacked the house of the enemy *daimyo*, and beheaded him. They had fulfilled their obligation to their dead lord and to their own honour, but they had offended against their obligation to the emperor and to the *shogun*. The only answer was a beautiful death. They all disembowelled themselves ceremonially, as was a *samurai*'s right.

The forty-seven *ronin* have a shrine of remembrance in a Tokyo suburb. The importance of their story lies in its popularity, as a clue to the kind of reassurance the Japanese people need to draw from their history. But it is not typical of the Tokugawa period, which was largely a time of peace. The *samurai* class turned their talents to administration. They became bureaucrats, on fixed stipends. The *samurai* still had the status, but the merchants, despite their lowly place in the feudal structure, had the money.

Money, in fact, had become increasingly important so that by the start of the nineteenth century its use had spread over the whole country, displacing barter. The financial power of the merchants became as significant as the administrative and martial power of the *samurai* class. Political and social stability allowed credit and trade to expand, unifying Japan as an economic entity. In the countryside the use of wages became widespread, and influential groups of rural merchants and landlords appeared. In the great cities of Edo, Osaka, Kyoto, and Nagasaki the foundations of financial and trading empires were being laid. Knowledge of modern Western ideas was sparse but not altogether absent. A small elite had acquired such knowledge through a tiny enclave of Dutch traders in Nagasaki, the only foreigners allowed to operate in Japan since the time of the Shimabara massacre. Japan, then, had already modified the feudal structure of society, at least in a de facto way, when the time came to face the next great shock to the social system.

The shock was provided by Commodore Matthew Perry and a squadron of American ships which sailed into Edo Bay in 1853. The Americans were seeking staging posts for their trade with China, and any other advantages that presented themselves. The Japanese gloomily signed treaties of amity and commerce with the United States and soon afterwards with other Western powers. The treaties contained unequal provisions of the kind the West had recently imposed on the tottering regime in imperial China.

This humiliation prompted a group within the Japanese elite to stage an almost bloodless revolution from the top, which ended the Tokugawa regime with the slogan "Revere the Emperor, expel the

barbarian". The main push for change came from the younger *samurai* and the new, rich class of rural merchants. In 1868, fifteen years after Commodore Perry's ominous visit, imperial rule was restored. The emperor, a young man called Meiji, was brought from Kyoto to Edo which was then renamed Tokyo.

Far from expelling the barbarians the new regime began almost at once to copy them and learn from them. The impulse behind the Meiji Restoration was not nostalgia for absolute imperial rule, which had been unknown for more than a thousand years. It was nationalism. The only way to express nationalism convincingly to the Japanese was, and to a smaller extent still is, through the mystically powerful institution of the emperor.

Shinto became the state cult, under state control. The divine descent of the imperial house was state dogma. A moderately liberal constitution was proclaimed containing provisions for elected assemblies and recognition of individual rights. From the late 1800s to the 1930s Japan performed prodigies of change, seeking a proper place in the world of modern nations. Political institutions, banking houses, industrial concerns, military organization, artistic styles, were all copied and adapted. Now the West became the fount of useful knowledge, as China had been a thousand years earlier. It looked like Westernization, but it was essentially modernization. It would have been impossible without the values of group cohesion and discipline which had been evolving since the first rough court assembled at Nara, and which had emerged as ideology under the Tokugawas. The dark side of this valuable coin appeared in the 1930s.

The world Japan had entered with such enthusiasm was a dangerous place, carved up by the tactics of economic cupidity and echoing with the rhetoric of high moral purpose. The Japanese acquired these skills, too. Already they had a small empire, which they realized was a necessary qualification for important nationhood, after territorial wars with Russia and China. Now a clique of militarists sought to add Manchuria to Taiwan and Korea. At home the *zaibatsu*, or monopoly cliques, controlled industry. Radical agitation was put down ruthlessly. The most extensive education system in Asia became a channel for indoctrination in nationalism and xenophobia based on racial purity and a vague but sinister interpretation of "the Japanese spirit". The sense of cosmic destiny grew, and was offended by what Japan believed was the reluctance of the Western nations to accept its proper place among the great powers. And in Southeast Asia an empire full of resources seemed there for the taking. Japan went to war.

The story of what happened then is well enough known. So is the fact that the code of Bushido was tarnished by the behaviour of some Japanese troops and celebrated honourably by the courage of others. It was difficult for the West to understand why the Japanese were so brave and so brutal. The bravery of the Japanese was the outcome of the *samurai* code, or a rather degenerate version of it, in which they had been so thoroughly indoctrinated. Even the suicide missions of the *kamikaze* pilots—young men riding the Divine Wind to a beautiful death—began not with orders from the High Command but with volunteers who asked to be allowed to die for Japan.

As for brutality, the ordinary Japanese soldier was brutalized by the treatment he received from his own officers. His food and medical resources were generally poor. He treated others the same way. Outside Japan he felt released from its rules of courtesy. He was also frightened by his contact with other societies, having been so tightly sealed inside his own. His indoctrination in the glories of the Japanese spirit led him to regard Asians who were not Japanese as lesser creatures—not the first time such a thing has happened in the history of empires. He was not reluctant to humiliate the strutting Europeans—especially prisoners of war who, by his own code, were men without honour. Explanations may not be a sufficient excuse. But then, all societies in war do some terrible things.

Right up to the moment when the first atomic bomb fell on Hiroshima on 6 August 1945, the Japanese propaganda machine had been assuring the people that the war was going according to plan. Every retreat was only an opportunity to come to closer grips with the enemy. There was talk of defending the sacred soil of Japan with bamboo spears, and no one doubted it. The Americans expected to be fighting from house to house from one end of Japan to the other. The

14, 15. The Emperor Meiji, as a young man, and his wife.

bomb on Hiroshima, and a second on Nagasaki three days later, changed all that at the cost of some 150,000 Japanese lives. On 14 August Japan capitulated. That may not be surprising in itself, in the face of a demonstration of such awful power, but two things about it are surprising, and instructive.

Firstly, the speed and completeness of the surrender. Everyone knew that surrender was a dishonourable thing for the Japanese, yet when the word was given they laid down their arms. Why? Because the word came from the emperor, and had to be obeyed. If the emperor had said "Die" they would have died. But he said "Surrender"—and they did. The emperor had given expression to a consensus among the ruling elite. There were some bitter-enders who wanted to fight on. The emperor had no power to impose his own view arbitrarily, but when he identified a consensus and put words to it his authority was unchallengeable. This has always been the Japanese way, even under the *shoguns*. There has never been a dictator in the Western sense in Japan.

The second interesting thing is what happened after the surrender. With hardly a backward glance the Japanese people turned away from years of indoctrination. They accepted that war was not the way to win a proper place—not that it was sinful and a cause for guilt, but that it was a failure and a cause for shame.

16. One ruined building in Hiroshima has been left as part of a peace park and memorial to the victims of the atomic holocaust on 6 August 1945.

17. Aspiring sumo wrestlers at a practice session in Tokyo.

During their benevolent if somewhat bemused post-war occupation—the MacArthur shogunate—the Americans imposed a more democratic constitution. It guaranteed individual liberties and rights, and also, uniquely, renounced Japan's right to wage war. The emperor was described merely as the "symbol of the state". Ultra-nationalists, and soon afterwards communists, were purged from positions of leadership and from the education system. America encouraged an economic recovery. The Japanese pulled themselves together, then they set out again to win the respect of the world—this time by peaceful means.

New technologies provided the means, but older social patterns provided the spirit, and still do, despite the seductions of Western management theory.

Dr. Sanai Mito, executive director, the Sharp Corporation:

To my mind, there are two schools of thought on management in this country. One is, so to say, the imported thoughts from the United States or from Europe. This school treats the employees rather as materials or machines, to my mind. The second school of thought treats the employees as human beings, and as members of the whole family. The company itself is thought to be like a big family and the one at the top, the president, is thought to be the father of the big family, and in that way we feel, and I myself personally feel, that the sense of responsibility of the employees has very much to do with a feeling of loyalty towards their father the president.

Outside working hours the ordinary man's friends tend to be the people he works with, very likely the ones who were his classmates at school or university. He is a member of a group first, and an individual second. At home father is the head of the family. Only recently has the Western word "Papa" begun to replace more formal and respectful Japanese terms, and then only in the cities. The housewife is not subservient entirely. Many men give their unopened pay packets to their wives and get some pocket money back. And the mother role is deeply respected in Japan. Father is not usually an autocrat; consensus operates in the family too, but there is no doubt about the pecking order.

Of course there are changes in attitudes and behaviour. Japan is just as much a part of the shifting international scene of sport, fashion, culture, and taste as any other rich and developed nation. But the continuities are there.

Very young children spend all their time with their mothers, much of it in close physical contact, strapped to her back. Their existence is bound up intimately with another person. That is where security and completeness are, not in individuality but in belonging. In early childhood the group means only warmth, indulgence, and enjoyment, but the realization that it means obligation as well is not far away. In kindergarten children are already in competition for places in the best universities. Some kindergartens even have entrance examinations. Success in student life reflects honour on the whole family. So does success in later life, and this depends heavily on education.

18. Tokyo children at kindergarten, where competition begins for place in the best schools and universities.

19. An assembly line on a huge scale—the Mitsubishi shipyard, Nagasaki (opposite).

Social mobility was possible even in Tokugawa times. A *samurai* family might sink into the lower orders through ill-fortune or foolishness, a merchant family might be promoted to *samurai* status through merit or even through bribery. Mobility up and down the social scale was perhaps not common, but it was possible. It is much easier for a modern Japanese family to rise in the social scale, since an industrial society as big and complex as Japan's implies some kind of meritocracy. The key is education—not only its quality, but also its provenance. A very bright boy with a first class degree will have even better prospects if the degree is from a highly regarded university. Japan's universities, like everything else, are understood to have a ranking order. Tokyo University is at the top. Throughout student life the pressure on children not to fail, for the sake of the family, is heavy, sometimes *too* heavy. Student suicides are not rare.

Nor are double suicides by lovers. This has been a favourite theme of Japanese fiction since Tokugawa times. Sometimes it may reflect the familiar conflict between obligation and human feelings, sometimes an attempt to forge a stainless union and live forever in the Pure Land of Buddhist doctrine.

One of the visible changes in Japan is a relaxation among young people of the formal rules of public behaviour; they touch each other more freely, strolling about hand in hand or cuddling in the parks. It is still very rare to see kissing in public, however. Despite the growth of the idea of romantic love, largely no doubt through the influence of Hollywood, many marriages are still arranged—if not by the family, then by marriage agencies of which Japan has several hundreds. It is not easy to establish new relationships outside the group, which is close and defensive. The group which determines social contact for millions of Japanese is a large and paternal corporation such as Mitsui, Nippon Steel, or Mitsubishi.

Father Bairy:

When a Japanese is introducing himself he does not say "I am John", or "I am Peter", or the equivalent, but he says "Mitsubishi"—the first word you hear is "Mitsubishi-no" ("of Mitsubishi"), then his name, Tanaka maybe, and then his first name is practically unknown. This introduction reveals precisely the way in which the Japanese is implicated in society. His home is Mitsubishi. The home we call home is just the sleeping quarters, but the centre of his life is in Mitsubishi, and this commitment is so total that he cannot think of any other possibility of getting in touch with people, except through an intermediary who would bridge the gap between the other one and himself. This explains the formalism of Japanese relations and also why the Japanese lack casualness in contracting friendships with foreigners.

This idea of the intermediary in social relationships has even received the ultimate accolade of the mass media—a television show of its own. For several years recently a Tokyo commercial station ran a programme devoted to introducing marriageable people to each other. It was very elaborate and technologically gimmicky, with a computer to select partners on the basis of age, interests, and so on. Hundreds of young (even not-so-young) people were involved, sitting bashfully in tiered ranks in the studio, or attending dances and parties organized by the station (and, of course, video-taped for use in the programme). So far as I know there is no record of the success rate of marriages arranged through the programme, but it may well be quite high. The people involved would very likely see nothing grotesque in the way they were paired off. It was simply necessary for them to use an intermediary to break out of their own small circle, and a computer, studio lights, and electronic cameras would not seem strange matchmakers in Tokyo, where fads and gimmickry flourish as they do in most huge and affluent cities. The fads are taken solemnly while they last. One marriage agency, indeed, had some success with a series of more or less nude weddings which it arranged as a promotional lark. The happy couple were not actually nude, but wore no more than imitation fig leaves and, for the bride, two other small, flower-shaped pieces of white brocade. The bare-breasted bridesmaids were models hired for the occasion. These occasions were called, interestingly, "germ-free" weddings. An unconscious echo, perhaps, of Shinto purification rites.

Other promotional exercises are intended more seriously. Religious and political movements come and go, seeking a way to reconcile the demands of a modern society using technologies based on logic and rational analysis, with the historical force of an agrarian culture based on group loyalties and emotion. One such group is Soka Gakkai, which claims ten million members and follows the teaching of the Nichiren Buddhist sect. The sect was founded in the thirteenth century by Nichiren, a monk with a fanatical zeal for his own view of the true Buddhism and a fierce intolerance of other views. Nichiren believed Japan was threatened by decadence within and aggression without. In general Soka Gakkai shares these views today. It is a highly sophisticated organization with its own daily newspaper and, until a recent split, its own political party. Soka Gakkai's recruiting is vigorous, its style intoxicating. It is given to huge rallies enlivened by drummers, clean-cut choirs, and modest dancing girls, and exhorted by arm-waving speakers. Its political views are highly conservative. It has branches in several other countries, including the United States and Australia. It believes, like Nichiren, that Japan will one day be the centre of a religious revival which will save the world and usher in the Millennium.

The fact is, I suspect, that the values of Japan are inimitable. Not for export. Everything comes in, not much goes out. Industrial products, of course—but what else? Zen Buddhism, appealing to intellectuals by discounting the intellect; martial arts such as *judo*; flower arranging, which used to calm the emotions of the *samurai*, to decorate middle-class coffee tables. All valuable things no doubt, but limited. Ideas which are really Japanese seem to lack universality.

Some difficulties flow from this—for instance, in dealings with other developed countries. Westerners look for long-term contracts full of fine print: a commitment of reason. The Japanese seek a more generalized relationship of trust: a commitment of feeling.

For the individual Japanese the world outside Japan is a frightening place. All the intricate social cues he has learned from childhood are worthless, because no one shares them. At home the Japanese have not resolved the conflict between change and continuity. Well—who has? But it seems to have peculiar poignancy here, where the need to belong is so great and the obligations of belonging are so heavy.

We began with a paradox. The answer turns out to be another. (That's very Zen!) It is this:

There is a word which recurs time and time again in Japanese literature and in art criticism as expressing something, for the Japanese, especially moving. It seems to me to fit the Japanese themselves, as a great nation in the community of nations, and as individuals despite their tight little groups in a crowded society.

The word is "lonely".

20. A busy shopping street—modern Japan is not all refinement and subtlety (left).
21. The quiet harmony of a temple pagoda roof against the evening sky, Nara (opposite).

2 Hong Kong and Singapore

Fragrant Harbour—Lion City

Tourists come to **Hong Kong**—more than a million of them every year—as though to a giant supermarket. If you have the money you can buy anything here. Salesmanship is aggressive. And why not? Tourists come here to spend, and what Hong Kong is about above all is free competition for money. The competition may occasionally have a note of desperation. An Australian visitor told me he was taken firmly by the arm and almost dragged from the pavement into a tailor's shop, and then was insulted when he insisted that he really didn't want to buy anything. To understand the urgency behind Hong Kong money-making, and in fact to understand why the place is there at all, we should begin some sixty-five kilometres away and four hundred years ago, in the tiny Portuguese settlement of Macau.

Macau, once a name to conjure with on the China coast, slumbers in old age now, nursing its memories at the mouth of the Pearl River. It was the first European settlement on the mainland of China, founded by the Portuguese in 1557, only sixty-five years after Columbus had sailed for the New World. It was a foot in the door of China: with the important trading city of Canton only eighty kilometres upstream. It was a staging post on the way to Japan to collect treasure and to save souls. The Portuguese and the Spanish, temporarily joined in one empire, established a missionary settlement in Nagasaki led for a time by St. Francis Xavier. Macau was an outpost of what was called, much later, European economic imperialism—a drab phrase for four hundred years of high adventure, faith, cant, self-sacrifice, and exploitation.

The Jesuit order brought faith and technology. The priests were entangled with traders' ambitions and government policy. The Jesuits, among their manifold talents, were excellent makers of cannon. A Chinese scholar remarked: "While Buddha came to China on white elephants, Christ was borne on cannonballs."

Macau's fortunes rose and fell as Portugal's did. By the eighteenth century opium-running had become the basis of trade between the

22. Trading junks at the mouth of the Pearl River, Macau.

West and China. Other powers forced themselves in—the Dutch, the Americans, and most notably the English. Opium became a national habit in China, and a source of huge profit to British India, which exported it. The English were ashamed of the opium trade and were very good at it, thus enriching both their consciences and the Treasury. To protect the trade, they acquired in 1841 an outpost of their own: the island of Hong Kong, on the far side of the Pearl River mouth. As the new British outpost began to flourish, Macau fell into a rather raffish decline. Its later history is enlivened by gambling casinos, a slightly mysterious trade in gold, and tourism.

Portuguese rule has been a polite fiction since the Chinese Cultural Revolution of the 1960s, when a communist veto power was imposed on legislation. These days there are no street parades to celebrate the Feast of St. John the Baptist, patron saint of the colony.

Macau is old, seedy, and highly picturesque. More than that, it is a monument to the first steps in a relationship between two cultures— that of China and that of Western Europe—in which each side misjudged and misunderstood the other with growing confidence. Macau is where the history is. The action, these days, is in the new, thrusting, and visually dramatic colony of Hong Kong.

23. The Portuguese atmosphere of a Macau street.

There was no nonsense about imperial mission when Hong Kong was established. It was a place to make as much money as possible as quickly as possible. It still is. But behind the fairy floss of the cut-price emporium there are now four and a half million people continuing the guarded confrontation of cultures that began centuries ago in Macau.

For most of the history of Hong Kong most of the people who lived there had come from somewhere else. They were traders, officials, soldiers, missionaries, but mostly refugees from China at various times and for various reasons. Now the proportions are changing. Slightly more than half the population were born in Hong Kong. But it is still an artificial society, and in some ways a very strange one. It is a British crown colony, and of course its government is British. But the basic fact about the place is that with heart, mind, and abacus Hong Kong is Chinese.

What is generally called simply Hong Kong is in fact three places— Hong Kong island itself; Kowloon, an urban area on the mainland; and the New Territories, a hilly peninsula between Kowloon and the border of Kwantung province in China.

It is still possible to find an ancient social structure in the New Territories, a tiny fossil of traditional Chinese rural life. For tourists it is charming, and for scholars it is a rich field of study. For the 98 per cent of Hong Kong's population who are Chinese the base-line for their values and social attitudes is preserved here, in the ancient rural

24. Between hills and harbour is the dynamic cityscape of Hong Kong.

system of kinship and lineage. The system has a long history. There are more than nine hundred million Chinese inside and outside China, but fewer than eight hundred surnames. Ties of kinship in the New Territories are powerful. They even have their monuments in the walled clan villages where everyone's surname is the same. The clan village of Kam Tin, for instance, where everyone is called Tang, has genealogical records going back for eight centuries.

25. A farmer using ancient methods in the New Territories.

The Confucian virtues of filial piety and reverance for ancestors are derided inside China. Outside it they are weakened by creeping Westernization. The clan villages of the New Territories, wedged between stern ideology and neon-lit temptation, are running out of time. But that is not to say by any means that the values and attitudes which have their roots there are no longer powerful.

Even the younger and better-educated generation pays some heed to Taoist spirits, ancestor cults, Buddhist gods of the Chinese tradition, and deities with various magical powers—all the inhabitants of the supernatural world of old China. This has less to do with mystical communion or a better life in the hereafter than it has to do with good fortune in this life. It is about the struggle for wealth, importance, success. In traditional China the gentry affected to despise the pursuit of money. But they were the ones who *had* the money and the status. The ordinary people of Hong Kong, for the most part, haven't much of either. They want both; that is why they came to Hong Kong.

26. Part of Hong Kong's central business district (above).

27. Here the business is all at street level—a walkway crowded with shoppers and sightseers (above right).

The commercial scene in the colony is vigorous from top to bottom. Much of it is underpinned by the ties of kinship which allow trust to be extended, and responsibility shared, within a code of ethics. What some societies call nepotism a Chinese may call fulfilling his obligations. The code of ethics operates internally, within known relationships, not externally towards strangers and foreigners. Business has a confident front. This does not necessarily mean it is doing well. There is a Chinese saying: "When business is bad, paint the counter." If a man can get rich quickly anywhere he can do it in Hong Kong. He can also get poor quickly. Free competition requires a gambler's instinct.

The values of old China are one thing. The values, and the policies, of new China are quite another. There is obviously a certain nervous tension involved for a European colony on the very coast of the People's Republic—especially when China's sufferance is tied, by historical finagling, to a particular date.

What Britain wanted when it acquired Hong Kong was a safe harbour. Hong Kong actually means "fragrant harbour"—but that was some time ago. Britain insisted, with gunboats and troops, on its right to continue the opium trade. Hong Kong Island and Kowloon were ceded to Britain by the tottering court of imperial China. The New

Territories, however, were leased from China in 1898. This lease will expire in 1997. Will China renew it? It might seem unlikely, ideologically. But there is more to it than ideology.

The theory, the hope, is that the success of Hong Kong's freewheeling economy makes it valuable not only to Britain, but also to China. The island was picked as a British outpost by one Captain Elliott, a naval officer. The choice of the barren island was unpopular in Britain, and poor Elliott was laughed into disgrace and exile as consul-general in Texas. They stopped laughing pretty quickly when the Taipans, or "great managers" such as Jardine and Matheson began to turn a handy profit. The Taipans or their successors, are still powerful. So are the nineteenth-century doctrines of laissez-faire economics. The colony is run in a businesslike way in the interests of businessmen.

Foreign correspondent and writer on Hong Kong, Richard Hughes:
The reason we exist is that we are so important to China. This "borrowed place on borrowed time" exists because they don't borrow money from here, they earn money. It's reliably estimated that they get about a million pounds a day in earnings that come through Hong Kong, either as trade or as overseas money, or as interest, and they use us as the entrepot. We suit them. They have not only got one big bank, the People's Bank opposite the old cricket ground, but they have also got four other banks and fifty department stores, a couple of insurance companies and a whole glut of shops, including some restaurants with Shanghai-type waitresses, making it completely commercialized communism. And we've got some very good, successful, loyal, Chinese communist millionaires.

The less sanguine British residents are fond of saying that if it wanted to, China could take Hong Kong with a telephone call. It is not an atmosphere to encourage long-term social vision. What is required is flexibility, and an eye to the main chance. Before World War II Hong Kong was the warehouse for the China trade. Then it languished under Japanese occupation. After the communist takeover in China it turned to manufacture—first textiles, then plastics and electronics. It acquired skilled labour in the thousands of refugees from Shanghai, as well as rich factory-owners and entrepreneurs and other sophisticated members of the commercial middle class.

Hong Kong has never had the social patterns of old China. It had no mandarins, the elite corps of bureaucrats. It had no gentry to speak of, and few scholars. The balance is changing after several generations of education, but many thousands of Hong Kong Chinese are still suffering the cultural shock of having to turn themselves from a rural peasantry into an urban proletariat.

Refugees still arrive, not all of them legally. One estimate says that illegal immigrants come in at the rate of about 35,000 a year. Some find shelter among the squatters still huddled in shacks on the hill-

28. Steep laneway through huddle of squatters' shacks on a Hong Kong hillside.
29. The "pigeon cages"— high-rise housing estates (right).

sides. Legal or illegal, the squatters are an embarrassment, but there is not room for everyone, yet, in the government's high-rise housing estates which the locals call "the pigeon cages".

Even for those who do make it to the high-rise blocks conditions are hardly luxurious. Extended family ties are difficult in small apartments. The Hong Kong Chinese do seem to have an extraordinary capacity to live their private lives in public, mentally shutting out the crowd, but that is an adaptation to crowded living, not a preference for it.

Peking regards Hong Kong officially as simply part of China, and has described the influx of people into Hong Kong as merely "population movement within Kwantung province". The British government has been obliged to restrict the flow. Even so, the pressure of population in a restricted space is extreme. People living in barely tolerable conditions look for ways of easing the pressure. Some of them are dangerous ways.

Drugs are a major problem—not only the opium smoked in seedy divans, but heroin too, and other killers. The administration has a new preventive service to try to cope. It also has an independent commission to attack bribery and corruption, the endemic Asian way of oiling the machinery of government and commerce.

30. View from the top of the jungle shows a rooftop school in a high-rise housing estate, Kowloon.

Among the major culprits in both areas, drugs and corruption, are the triads or secret societies, a degenerate hangover from regional self-protection movements in old China. The triads are especially strong in a part of Kowloon known as the Walled City. This small, unsavoury area is not actually walled, but is almost surrounded by tightly packed, open-fronted shops in narrow, twisting lanes. It is of no obvious importance to anyone, yet it has a peculiar place in the tangle of disputation about leases and sovereignty which bedevils Hong Kong. Peking claims the area as former diplomatic territory. The secret societies take advantage of the doubt. Until recently, when raids began on drug dens, the authorities hesitated to exert their powers in the Walled City. It is a grotesque example of the heart of Hong Kong's social difficulties—sensitivity to what China thinks.

Merely by looking around the colony—at the contrast, say, between The Peak residential area and the high-rise blocks—anyone can see that there is a huge gap between the top and the bottom of the society. The government of the colony, apparently humane and doing its best, is autocratic. The governor has the advice of an executive council and a legislative council. None of the members is elected. The urban council has twelve elected members out of twenty-four, but the voting franchise is very restricted. One might expect this to have produced a volatile political situation, with popular cries for some dramatic changes. But not so. There are communists in the colony, and supporters of the Taiwan Nationalist regime, and views in between. There have been occasional troubles. In 1967 there were serious riots instigated and encouraged by the communists, but they were a spillover of the cultural revolution in Canton. On the whole there seems to have been a tacit understanding that a vigorous political life in Hong Kong would be too provocative to Peking. Hong Kong has so far chosen to remain politically neuter. It may not be natural, but it's safe.

For their part, the British adopt a low profile. There is not much pomp and circumstance. The government offers no ideology, no social message, except for watchwords like progress, law and order, and social harmony. For most of the twenty-five thousand Europeans in the colony Hong Kong is not home, but somewhere to have a career or a business, and count the money.

There are some voices calling for more commitment to Hong Kong as home. The articulate ones are likely to be products of the better private schools and of Hong Kong University where a Western education is supposed to encourage analysis and enquiry. But even there modern notions about democracy come up against a mood of resignation which is much older. Among a group of students with whom I had a long conversation, most wanted changes of various kinds but believed that pressures from China would make them impossible. One retailed the orthodox Peking line that Hong Kong was part of China. Only one had really positive views about a radical change in the system.

Mrs. Lui Fung Mei Yee, law student:

What I would like to see is Hong Kong becoming an independent state with its own political and legal system. I would think that if China were to take back Hong Kong it would raise big problems, complicated problems with the four and a half million people involved, the question of adapting the style of living, the ideas, and so on. On the other hand I wouldn't like to see Hong Kong remaining as a colony because it means that people will still have that sense of insecurity where everybody is looking for a sure investment and nobody wants to contribute to Hong Kong and build up a permanent home there. So what I want is an independent state just like Singapore.

The conventional wisdom is that while China might be able to tolerate a colony which it finds useful, and which everyone knows it could snuff out at whim, it would find it much harder to tolerate an independent state on what Peking insists is its own territory. I must say I share that view. At the same time, as Mrs. Lui says, China would face enormous difficulties in absorbing the Hong Kong population of private entrepreneurs and, in Peking terms, their lackeys. A policy of masterly political inaction seems likely to continue.

There is a Chinese saying that wealth does not cross three generations. Hong Kong did not invent the idea of short-term gains and
fancy footwork in business, but it allows this way of life to flourish in
a way impossible inside China. There is a growing Chinese middle
class of professionals, businessmen, and entrepreneurs, many of them
refugees from Shanghai where capitalist enterprise held sway until
1949. They have adopted some Western trappings, turning the ac-
quisition of face into a familiar status game.

Richard Hughes:

There is quite an aristocratic element here of very wealthy Chinese who
live in extraordinarily luxurious circumstances. They like to send their
families overseas for education. They gain great face in the Western style
by having huge cars. They gain Chinese face by belonging to several clubs,
and by giving money on festival days, more than a neighbour if they can.
In the old days they used to keep two concubines instead of one; it was a
good way of keeping ahead of the Wongs. They live very well, are very
hospitable, and sometimes very snobbish.

Success in Hong Kong is in being seen to be successful. It is not
alone in that. In other societies, however, status can come from a
well-publicized involvement in cultural affairs. The art gallery and
the concert hall can take over as a focus of interest from "My son, the
doctor". The difficulty with that in Hong Kong is, which culture?

31. A mansion in an idyll
setting gives some idea of th
wealth at the top end of
Hong Kong society.

32. Boy on a house-boat, eking out a living from day to day.

33. Polo—part of the thriving sporting life for British expatriates, a world away from the lower rungs of Hong Kong's population.

34. Brightly painted members of traditional Chinese opera troupe which, with government support, tours the housing estates.

Some of the expression of Chineseness is bound up with religion, superstition, and myth. Like the dragon boat festival, which annually commemorates the death of a court official who drowned himself in despair at the corruption of the court in fourth-century China. It is a tourist draw, but also a connection with a cultural tradition. So is traditional Chinese opera, a sad remnant of a higher cultural form, in shrill but vain competition with colour television. Certainly crowds still turn out to watch government-supported troupes performing at open-air theatres in the apartment block areas, but according to my own observation they are mostly of middle age and above. It is an expression of nostalgia for a China that is gone, and maybe never existed. As a cultural form it is dead. In looking for new forms Hong Kong has problems.

The film magnate, Mr. Run Run Shaw:

To a certain extent you can say that we have a touch of the feeling of a cultural desert, the reason being that after all the population in Hong Kong came from different parts of China. People had to settle down, and we have no history of cultural background. But now people are settling down, they are doing good business, their living is very comfortable, and of course they need cultural activities to improve their living and their interest and they are beginning to form all sorts of cultural associations.

Hong Kong remains culturally ambivalent. Ironically, it is a great exporter of culture, of a sort. It is the fount of most films for the overseas Chinese scattered through the countries of the region. There are costume melodramas, romantic melodramas, and kung fu. It is all assertively Chinese—not ideological, just ethnic, and commercial. Like Hong Kong itself.

The people of Hong Kong are proud of China but choose not to live in it. They are proud of their race but without a living culture to express it. They live in a place they are unable to govern. What else is there to do but make the best of it? Make money. If you are being paid, smile. Survive.

35. Buildings from the colonial era are now dwarfed by the modern business empire of Singapore city. (Photograph by courtesy of the Singapore Tourist Promotion Board.)

Singapore was acquired on the initiative of one man, Stamford Raffles, as Hong Kong was acquired on the whim of Captain Elliott. Again like Hong Kong, Singapore is basically Chinese, a small, crowded island, a centre of tourism and trade. The similarities are obvious, and misleading. It is a very different place.

Singapore is an independent city state. Its Chinese are *overseas* Chinese a long way from China (which most of them have never seen) and potentially vulnerable in the middle of a Malay world. The population of about two and a quarter millions includes two significant racial minorities. Fifteen per cent are Malays and 7 per cent are Indians. Survival here is not a matter of being politically neuter. Commitment is encouraged, so long as it is commitment to the right idea: a non-communist, mildly socialist state depending on capitalist enterprise. Singapore was part of Malaysia for two years. It was asked to leave in 1965, basically because of racial tensions.

As an independent state Singapore is a social laboratory. To survive it has to make multi-racialism work.

The first residents were the Malays. A fishing settlement on the island is mentioned in Chinese records in the early centuries of the Christian era. It was called Temasek—Sea Town. It fell under the control from time to time of the kings of Siam and the empires of Sumatra and Java. Culturally, like other Malays, its people were influenced by Indian traders, adopting first Hinduism and Buddhism and later Islam. A sizeable township on the island was destroyed in the fourteenth century, but not before a Sumatran prince, mistaking a tiger for a lion, had renamed the place Singa Pura—the Lion City.

36. A Malay fisherman casts his net in a pattern of life unchanged for many centuries.

When the British arrived at the start of last century there were a few hundred Malay fishermen and pirates and a small group of Chinese farmers.

Nowadays the Malays, in their kampongs (villages) or in the city, are part of the modern society. But in economic terms they have tended to fall into the lower part. One view is that there is something in Malay culture which inclines them to be non-competitive.

Professor S.H. Alatas, head of the department of Malay Studies, University of Singapore:

I don't think that view is correct. As far as the Malay culture is concerned we have plenty of historical evidence pointing in the opposite direction. Malays have been encouraged by their culture to go into business, to go into trade, to acquire knowledge and education, and they have been encouraged culturally also to have discipline, a sense of organization. They have built up magnificent states in the past, and they have engaged in very great international trade ... so this view is completely incorrect. [The chapter on Malaysia further discusses this point.]

37. The reality of existence at the bottom of the heap—a Malay kampong, Singapore island.

Like other Singaporeans the Malays are urged towards prudence and economy. Their own leaders have suggested, for instance, that they should have less elaborate weddings and should spend their money where it matters. What matters is careful housekeeping, and development—although Singapore is not beyond a little honest sentiment. Developers seem intent on rebuilding the whole city in one

generation, but so far at any rate they have not laid hands on one of the world's great hotels, the Raffles. It is rather tired now, perhaps, but still has a certain air. It is famous as an example of the high style of British colonialism, which is somewhat odd since it was built, in 1890s, in the French Renaissance manner by three Armenians. It was well named. Whatever other qualities the enigmatic Thomas Stamford Raffles might have had, the man had style. And he knew what he wanted.

Raffles was seeking "one fine port", he said, "to destroy the spell of Dutch monopoly" over trade in the area. In 1819 he came over from Bencoolen, a small British settlement over which he presided in Sumatra, and acquired rights to build a trading settlement on the island and to control the port. To do this Raffles arbitrarily recognized one of two disputants for the sultan's throne in the neighbouring state of Johore, which claimed sovereignty over Singapore, and provided annuities for the sultan and one of his supporters. The East India Company, which employed Raffles, the British government, and the Dutch, were all very angry. The Dutch were soothed with concessions elsewhere, including the surrender to them of Britain's small Bencoolen settlement in Sumatra, and the others were quickly soothed with success. Singapore's crucial position between the Indian Ocean and the China sea gave it enormous advantages. Within a few years it

38. The Raffles Hotel, a reminder of what colonialism meant—to the British (above). (Photograph by courtesy of the Singapore Tourist Promotion Board.)

39. The seedy charm of Singapore's Chinatown (opposite). (Photograph by courtesy of the Singapore Tourist Promotion Board.)

was the trading centre of south eastern Asia. It became a staging post for opium on the way to China, and for tea and silk on the way back. As its fortunes rose so did its need for labour. China supplied it.

The same poverty and rebellion which sent many thousands fleeing from southern China to Hong Kong in the middle of last century sent thousands also to Singapore. "My industrious Chinese" Raffles called them. So long as they were industrious they were largely left alone to live as they liked. But progress catches up. Now Chinatown is being demolished. Tourists will be sorry to see it go, and so will some of the old people who live there. For young Singaporeans, however, it is not what modern living is about. Its mixture of intimacy and picturesque squalor does not fit the "Rugged Society" the government says it is building. Nor do some of the old, traditional attitudes that go with it. Although some of those old attitudes could be pretty rugged.

The Chinese were terrorized by their own triads, the secret societies, in the early days. There were savage triad wars. Clan and regional loyalties could be explosive when mixed. The triads still survive—and not only in Chinatown—in protection rackets and other kinds of thuggery. There are more respectable survivals from early times: obligations to family and kinfolk, reverence for ancestors and respect for the old, and pride in simply being Chinese. Some of these things, especially the last, sit awkwardly in a multi-racial society. There are attempts to adjust some Chinese attitudes to life—and to death also.

Around Sago Lane are the last of Chinatown's death houses. Upstairs are old Chinese who have gone there to die, some because they had nowhere else to go, others because they were living with their children and to die at home would bring bad luck to the household. Downstairs are the undertakers, the coffin-makers, and the makers of funeral furnishings. These furnishings—food utensils, servants, model houses, carriages—are made of paper. They have to burn so as to accompany the departing spirit and ensure an arrival in some style in the next world. Chinese are encouraged to opt for cremation instead of burial, to conserve the island's scarce supply of fresh land. (This does not apply to the Muslim Malays, whose religion requires burial).

40, 41. Young and old Chinese women, Singapore.

42. One of Singapore's high-rise housing estates.

There are attempts to discourage elaborate funerals, of which the Chinese are fond. They involve much expense—not only to the bereaved but also to the guests at the ceremony. It is a serious loss of face not to make a substantial donation to speed a dead friend safely on his way, and people often go heavily into debt to do it. Whether such traditional ways should change or not depends on what you think is important.

Whatever else goes, the temples will stay, with their eclectic variety of gods. The beliefs and values springing from a rural peasantry somehow have to adapt to a modern, technological, urban state. No one knows how long it will take. It is all part of the Singapore experiment. Divisions of dialect and regional Chinese loyalties and divisions between the English-educated Chinese elite and the rest, become less important as identification with Singapore becomes more important.

About a quarter of the population is somewhere in the education system. Except for about 40 per cent of the old people, almost everyone is literate. All children learn Malay—the national language—and one other language.

The high-rise estates of apartment blocks (cleaner and more attractively planned than most in Hong Kong) are a part of the social laboratory. They face problems of crowded loneliness, depression, drugs, crime, and youthful mischief common to such estates everywhere. They also contain a planned racial mixture, as part of government policy. The pressure is on the Chinese to become less assertively Chinese, less exclusive than Chinese are elsewhere.

The last of the major racial groups to arrive in any numbers were the Indians, the great majority of them from southern India. There were some Muslims, Sikhs, and other groups, but most were Hindus. They still have elaborately decorated temples in which Vishnu the Preserver, Shiva the Destroyer, and Brahma the Creator claim allegiance. Some of the more orthodox Hindus still embrace the caste system, although this seems not to be very significant in Singapore.

Like the Chinese, the Indians came in waves. A few came even before the British had formally founded the Straits settlements of Penang, Malacca, and Singapore. Some came in the early colonial days as convict labour. The big wave came at the beginning of this century with the start of the rubber plantations. Most of the Indians who came then intended to return home. Many did, but many stayed. In Singapore their descendants quickly developed an English-educated upper class prominent in the professions, especially the law. A strong middle class developed, owning shops and businesses. A significant number proved to be adept at handling money—lending it, exchanging it, and making it.

Those skills are very Singaporean. The city state depends more than most on a reputation for honest financial dexterity. It has little margin for error, having no resources but its skills and the advantage of being where it is. An Asian dollar bank is part of the policy of development as the trading and financial centre for the whole region—in competition, to some extent, with Hong Kong. These policies are carried on within a political framework of authority inherited from the British, supervised by a highly professional elite almost entirely English-educated.

Japanese occupation in the 1940s destroyed the myth of white supremacy, if indeed anyone but the white man had ever believed it. It did not destroy a belief among the elites in the value of Western forms of government and law. These ideals have been modifed, here and there, in the Singapore experiment. There have been detentions without trial, and there are political prisoners. Opposition is not illegal, but demoralized. Newspapers are licensed and criticism is muted. Free-for-all politics which might allow communism a foothold, or vigorous debate which might inflame racial antipathies, are thought to be luxuries Singapore cannot afford. The emphasis is on discipline and efficiency.

Professor Alatas:

Singapore cannot afford to have a bad government—a bad government being one that tolerates corruption and inefficiency. If corruption is tolerated it will have serious repercussions on Singapore's development. For instance it will take away confidence in the institutions, it will probably scare away finance from capital investment, the banking system will suffer. Aside from the international consequences of corruption there is the matter of internal disruption. Corruption would cause serious internal disruption in Singapore society.

The point of this kind of concern is the danger that a really serious corruption scandal, or even a regular series of small ones, would quickly be translated in the popular mind into racial terms. Most of the big money in Singapore is, of course, in Chinese hands. Most officials are Chinese, simply as a result of population arithmetic. Any breath of "bought officials" of the kind common in some other countries would be racially inflammatory.

The encouragement of fellow-feeling between the races, and the reduction of points of friction, are constant preoccupations in Singapore. This is a matter of some delicacy, since too heavy-handed an approach might create exactly those tensions it was supposed to remove. Two interesting approaches to the problem are being made at the cultural level. The government-run Radio Singapore is trying to encourage listeners to develop an interest in the music and folk tales of all the ethnic groups, not just the one they belong to. The hope is that in the longer term this cross-cultural fertilization might lead to an identifiably Singaporean culture.

43. Indian girl (far left). (Photograph by courtesy of the Singapore Tourist Promotion Board.) **44.** Elaborately decorated Indian Hindu temple, Singapore.

This is also the ambition of the People's Association, a statutory body which has nearly two hundred community centres throughout the island. I watched rehearsals for a cultural display which included Malay dances, Indian dances, traditional Chinese orchestra, and Scottish Highland dances performed rather bashfully by Indian girls wearing kilts. The People's Association says it is not trying to impose any cultural pattern, but is hoping one will emerge through encouraging all strands by organization and participation.

Singapore is a participating society, a society of organizations. The People's Association is probably the biggest, with voluntary service, cultural, and sporting groups of all kinds. It provides, it says, a two-way channel between government and people. What comes up, presumably, is some indication of feeling at the grass roots. What goes down is inspiration, advice, exhortation. Much of it has to do with cleanliness, morality, community spirit, and national consciousness. The campaign seems to be having effect. Singapore is very clean. Everything works. Taxi drivers and others who come into contact with strangers are eager to extol the virtues of their little society and to hear them praised. There are dissenting voices, but they speak *sotto voce*. Some students resent official authoritarianism, but if they want to hold places in the university they do well to keep such views to themselves. Determination, self-reliance, and discipline are stern virtues; but survival, the government reminds everyone constantly, is a serious business.

Singapore and Hong Kong, both so delicately placed, are object lessons in the art of improbable survival. They have gone different ways and become very different places, under the pressures of history and circumstance. But in the end they share, and depend on, the cultural heritage of the Chinese people.

Hong Kong, without much sense of popular commitment, and Singapore, urgently requiring it, are both governed by small, professional ruling elites in undisputed control. Neither could survive without the readiness of the Chinese people, demonstrated over hundreds of generations, to accept elite power as a proper way of life and government.

It's an irony of cultural continuity that two such dissimilar societies should be the joint heirs of the long tradition of the mandarins.

45. Determined expressions worn by girl members of a Singapore youth organization during the National Day parade.

3 Indonesia

Unity in Diversity
(*Bhinneka tunggal ika*)

Every year on 17 August Indonesians from every part of their huge chain of islands gather to celebrate the most important thing they hold in common—national independence. Troops, marching youths, and decorated floats from every region pass in review before the president and enormous crowds. They are commemorating the date in 1945 on which Indonesia declared its independence from Dutch colonial rule. There were four more years of armed struggle and negotiation to pass before independence was formally recognized, but that is a matter for lawyers and history books. August 17 is the date for the people, for the emotions.

Nationalism is a suspect emotion these days, at least among intellectual groups in those societies which are fortunate enough to be able to take their nationhood and their sense of unity for granted. That is not true of the Third World in general, and it is certainly not true of Indonesia, where a real sense of unity, of national consciousness, is still not a fact, only an ambition. The national motto, "Unity in Diversity", expresses that ambition.

As well as a national motto, the Indonesians have an official statement of the "philosophical basis" of the republic, laid down by Dr. Sukarno in 1945. It is called *Panca Sila*—Five Principles. They are: belief in one god; humanity; nationalism; representative government; social justice. It is all at a very high level of abstraction. For thirty years Indonesian politicians and intellectuals have been trying to bring it down to earth and agree on what it means. They have not succeeded yet; but *Panca Sila* is powerful, apparently. It is referred to—appealed to—frequently at all levels, from presidential speeches to editorials in little country newspapers. The point of such a bland incantation may not be immediately obvious. The point is reassurance.

A nation of 125 million people living on three thousand islands with some three hundred ethnic groups and nearly as many languages, needs all the reassurance it can get that it is, in fact, one nation. *Panca Sila* is a symbol, a talisman. Indonesians still feel the pull between national pride and regional culture. It would be extraor-

46—48. Three faces of Jakarta's National Independence Day parade: a children's choir sings patriotic songs, a band marches, and the people watch.

dinary if they did not. Their diversity has very deep roots, in the different ways people see their relationship with the world and with each other, and, of course, with their god.

Indonesia is statistically a Muslim country. More than 90 per cent of the population regard themselves as Muslims, but Islamic fervour is by no means uniform. It is strongest where Islam first came in—in Aceh, on the northern tip of the island of Sumatra. Settlement in Aceh is very old. Those assiduous diary-keepers, the Chinese, have court records noting that one of their trading fleets visited Aceh in the first one or two decades of the Christian era. The bedrock of Indonesian civilization may already have been laid by that time: a complicated system of custom and ceremonial, based on spirit and ancestor worship and on the needs of the local communities for some kind of discipline and organization. But it was small-scale organization, based on the fishing village or the rice-paddy.

What happened over the next several hundred years was quite dramatic: the emergence of highly sophisticated societies in Sumatra and Java, exerting influence over wide areas of what we now call Southeast Asia. What made all this possible was what came into Aceh on the winds of the monsoon: influence from India.

The peaceful extension of Indian Hindu and Buddhist influence spread across most of the Indonesian archipelago and the Malay peninsula, and lasted for fourteen centuries. It left a significant residue in Indonesian life and thought, but it was overlaid by the spread of Islam.

Marco Polo mentions a Muslim city in north Sumatra in 1292. The faith was brought by Indians, Persians, and later Arabs. The heyday of the first Indonesian Muslim state, Aceh, came in the sixteenth and seventeenth centuries. It was begun unwittingly by the Portuguese, who captured the trading port of Malacca on the Malay peninsula in 1511. Many rich Muslim traders fled to Aceh, taking their trade and their money with them. By the early seventeenth century the Acehnese under their most famous leader, Sultan Iskander Muda, controlled not only most of north Sumatra but a large part of the Malay peninsula as well. Iskander Muda died in 1636. His successor died only five years later. The next four Acehnese rulers were women—a brief resurgence of the earlier matriarchy of north Sumatra.

After fighting off Acehnese attacks on Malacca several times, the Portuguese attacked Aceh itself. They gained a foothold, despite a fierce resistance including artillery pieces sent to Aceh by their Muslim brothers in Turkey. The Portuguese put up a fort and tried to bring the Acehnese people to heel. They did not have much success. No one ever has. The characteristics for which the Acehnese are

49. Animals graze in the unkempt Dutch cemetery in Banda Aceh, northern Sumatra.

known today were already apparent then—strict Islamic fervour, a martial spirit, and a rather prickly sense of independence. Their empire and wealth declined, however, when the next power in the land, the Dutch, set up a trading monopoly.

The Netherlands' long connection with what they called the East Indies began in 1596 when four ships under the command of Cornelius de Houtman sailed down the Sumatran coast to Java. De Houtman sailed around the Indonesian islands for three years, setting up trading contacts and even signing a treaty with a ruler in northern Java. Almost everywhere the local people welcomed him. In Aceh, they killed him.

The Dutch finally subdued Aceh. It took them three hundred years to do it. The final campaign, the Aceh War, lasted for thirty years into the start of this century. There is a Dutch cemetery in the regional capital, Banda Aceh, full of the sad debris of empire. As well as the tombs of senior officers and the graves of government servants, there are many graves of children. The area was heavily malarial. At the entrance is a dilapidated archway bearing a roll of honour of the names of those killed in the Aceh War. It is a memorial also to the lack of a sense of unity among the Indonesian people, that fatal flaw which allowed the Dutch to rule for so long. Most of the troops who finally subdued Aceh were not Dutch at all, but mercenaries from Java and other islands.

A sense of difference remains with the Acehnese. Aceh was one of several centres of bloody rebellion against the central Indonesian government in the late 1950s, led by Muslim thugs called Darul Islam. In 1968 the provincial legislature enacted Islamic law within Aceh province. Jakarta was less than delighted, but smiled bravely. There has been pressure from Aceh from time to time for the whole of Indonesia to become an official Islamic state, like Malaysia. The idea is not popular with most of their fellow Indonesians. The Acehnese are not very tolerant of the more easy-going Muslims in other regions, nor for that matter are they notably tolerant of other religions.

Indonesia's official policy is religious freedom and tolerance. The first of the five principles of *Panca Sila* is belief in one god, but the freedom to choose which kind of belief is guaranteed in the constitution. This has not prevented trouble between Muslims and Christians, of whom Indonesia has several millions. There has been violence over religion in more than one province, but the most serious has been in Aceh. A Christian church was sacked and burned on the west coast of the province as recently as 1967. The idea of the *Jehad*, or holy war in which death ensures an easy passage to paradise, receded in Aceh only within living memory, if in fact it is quite gone even now.

Just as the mosque dominates Banda Aceh, so Islam dominates the whole life of the Acehnese. This can be suffocating. There is a constant stream of young people from Aceh to Jakarta and the bright lights and the promise, up to a point, of a freer intellectual life.

In contrast to the Acehnese, the Minangkabau people of West Sumatra have not allowed Islam to override completely the earlier values embodied in *adat*, the law based on custom and tradition, although they have been Muslims for three centuries. In their villages in highland valleys running down to the coast the Minangkabau still build elaborate houses with roofs curved to echo the shape of buffalo horns. Minangkabau means "victorious buffalo". It refers to a legendary battle between champion buffalo which settled an argument about who should rule the local people in very early times. Like most race mythology, whether or not it is factual is beside the point. It says something important about the Minangkabau people. The buffalo which lost the fight was one belonging to an ambitious prince. The one which won had been chosen by a representative council as the champion of the people. The cultural heritage which the Minangkabau bring to Indonesia is one of strong individualism and a fierce pride in government by consent.

0. The mosque, Banda Aceh, centre of a strict and traditional interpretation of Islam.

51. Inside the Banda Aceh mosque.

Islam has found a way to live harmoniously with the Minangkabau matrilineal social system. The lines of descent and inheritance still pass through the women. Relationships among the Minangkabau are notoriously complicated, and the despair of outside lawyers. The head of the family is the mother's eldest brother. Social status depends on the uncle-nephew relationship, but the father-son relationship is the one supposed to control discipline. These interlocking relationships may mean that all the inhabitants of a village are related to each other in one way or another. The society is closely knit—a little too closely for comfort, perhaps.

For centuries young Minangkabau men have left their villages to seek fame and fortune in the cities of West Sumatra and even further afield. The tradition of voluntary migration is called *merantau*. This used to mean that when a man had proved himself he returned to his village and settled down. Gradually the pattern changed, until most men who left, left for ever. One researcher estimates that in the 1950s there were as many Minangkabau outside West Sumatra as there were inside.

The Minangkabau are a highly individualistic people, voluble, argumentative, intellectually lively. They have made a contribution far beyond their numbers to government, the arts, and scholarship in modern Indonesia, but at some cost to their own society.

Islam among the Minangkabau has tended to be orthodox in religious terms, but socially radical. The Minangkabau supported a rebellion against the Jakarta government in the late 1950s. They are not an easy people to govern. This has something to do with their concept of authority, developed over centuries in their own culture. Villagers obeyed the *penghulu*, the head of a group of villages under customary law, but the relationship was not one-way. The *penghulu* had no absolute personal power. His right to lead was based on the consensus of his small world. The lowly individual was not only the object but also the ultimate source of authority. A very modern view, but to the Minangkabau a very old one. Ideas about the legitimacy of authority, about who has the right to rule, about the very nature of power, are quite different elsewhere.

In central Java, about forty kilometres from the ancient city of Jogjakarta, is one of the wonders of Asia: the Buddhist temple of Borobudur. This massive pile is built like a carapace around a hill rising out of paddy fields and coconut groves. It is best seen at dawn, when mist still curls between the coconut palms and the sunlight touches the old stone softly.

52. Traditional Minangkabau house, with roof lines reflecting the curve of buffalo horns (far left).
53. Women working a village rice mill in Minangkabau country.

54. Minangkabau men off on a wild boar hunt near Bukit Tinggi (far left).
55. Minangkabau women drying rice in the hills inland from Padang, central Sumatra.

At present however (and probably until close to 1980) the impact of the scene is spoiled by a spindly yellow crane and a push of bulldozers, part of an internationally funded attempt to prevent Borobudur from collapsing—or, rather, from exploding. It seems that the outward pressure of the imprisoned earth threatens to burst its stone skin.

56. Borobudur temple's highest terrace, representing the sphere of formlessness. The Buddha figure was originally veiled, like the many others, by stone latticework.

Borobudur was built in the ninth century. It languished and was overgrown (or even, according to some scholars, was buried by devotees) about the year 1000, when the centre of power shifted to East Java and Islam began to penetrate. It was excavated and partly restored early last century.

The edifice is in the form of a pointed dome, or stupa, on a terraced, four-sided, pyramidal base. The base is 120 metres square; the whole edifice is 42 metres high. There are six square terraces topped by three round ones, with a crowning stupa. The levels are divided into the spheres into which Buddhist teaching divides life. At the bottom is the sphere of desire, symbolizing man's captivity by his senses: in the middle the sphere of form symbolizes Buddha's quest for enlightenment: and at the top the pilgrim is supposed to find at least an inkling of enlightenment.

In other words, Borodubur is an attempt to express in stone a view of what the world is all about. There are nearly three thousand panels of carved doctrine and decoration on the way up from bottom to top. At the top there is very little decoration—this is the sphere of formlessness which symbolizes spiritual truth, free of corruption and error. But there is not the dramatic abandonment of "the world, the flesh and the Devil" to be found in Christian doctrine, for this Buddhism teaches the unity of the whole cosmos: the difference between the bottom state and the enlightenment at the top is not a difference in the real state of the world, only in our perception of it. It's an elegant view, and Borodubur expresses it beautifully. The temple was built three hundred years before the Khmers built Angkor Wat, and four hundred years before many of the great cathedrals of Europe. Every stone breathes subtlety and sophistication. The cultural history of Java is long, rich, and complex. It is a culture of princes—a culture of power.

7. Another sunrise warms the stone of a Buddha who has been smiling gently at Borobudur for a thousand years (far left).

8. Detail of a bas-relief shows how the stone blocks of Borobudur are being forced apart by pressure from inside the great monument.

Borodubur was built by the rulers of the Hindu-Buddhist kingdom of Mataram, which flourished from the eighth to about the fourteenth century. They had help from their relatives the rulers of the powerful Sumatran empire of Sri Vijaya, which rose and fell over roughly the same period. Sri Vijaya was a centre of Buddhist learning with scholars and students from as far away as China.

The kingdom of Majapahit, founded in 1293, produced what Indonesians now regard as the golden age of Javanese culture. Before its final collapse in the sixteenth century its rulers turned to Islam. The last Javanese power was the second kingdom to be called Mataram, this time a Muslim one. It lasted from the sixteenth century to the eighteenth, when the Dutch finally gained control.

Unlike the Acehnese, influenced by generations of foreign traders and international notions of commercial interest, and unlike the Minangkabau, with a local culture emphasizing individuality and a kind of democratic spirit, the central Javanese society was formed by centuries of settled, inland agriculture. The system of authority was a simple hierarchy with a king at the top, a class of aristocratic warriors and bureaucrats in the middle, and the peasants at the bottom. Religion was set down, and remains today, in layers. At the bottom, no one knows how old, are the spirits of place, seasons, and the elements, who are conjured by magic. Next come the gods of the Hindu and Buddhist traditions, residents of Indonesia now for a thousand years. The top layer is Islam, bringing codified laws, an appeal to reason, and a call for discipline. The vast majority of Javanese are Muslim, statistically. But when the crop fails or some crisis threatens the family an appeal for help is likely to go not to Allah and his Prophet, but to the *dukun*, the village magician.

59. A pavilion in the *krator* (palace of the sultan), Jogjakarta.

The way of legitimizing the authority of the rulers has changed many times, from unashamed brute force, through the god-king of the Hindus, to the faithful servant of Allah, to the winner of an election, to the appointee of the generals. The idea of what it is that *makes* a ruler—his power—has been persistent through Javanese history. The style which was believed to show the possession of power is still reflected in, for instance, the now rather seedy elegance of the *kraton*, the palace of the sultan of Jogjakarta. The style became identified with the Javanese aristocrats called the *priyayi*, who provided the court retainers and administrators. It required smoothness, an unhurried pace, quietness of mind.

60. Dressed in the traditional batik design of central Java this man is an official of the court of the sultan of Jogjakarta.

According to the American scholar Benedict R. O'G. Anderson,* power was thought by the Javanese to be existential, an actual thing which could be gained, possessed, or lost. There was only a finite amount of it in the world, so that one man's gain of power was another's loss. One way of demonstrating the possession of power was through sexual prowess. The sultan who built the old Water Palace in Jogjakarta demonstrated his virility regularly, so it is said, by picking a maiden out of the swimming pool and having his royal way in the pavilion nearby. Water, an ancient symbol of power, flowed in a stream beneath the royal bed.

61. The pavilion and bathing pool in the old Water Palace, Jogjakarta.

---

* In Claire Holt, ed., *Culture and Politics in Indonesia* (Ithaca: Cornell University Press, 1972).

The shadow plays which are still widely popular in the countryside preserve the concept of power. The stories of the *wayang kulit*, the leather puppets, are from the Hindu Ramayana and Mahabaratha, much reworked into Javanese lore but still celebrating the god-king, the just prince, and their epic battles with the powers of darkness. *Wayang* puppet-masters themselves are powerful. A performance often lasts until dawn, but the audience knows that so long as it stays within the charmed circle of the puppet-master's power it is safe from the demons and evil spirits which are abroad in rural Java by night. This attitude to power spills over easily into fetishism. The Javanese are great wearers of charms and amulets said to possess protective powers. More classically, power has resided throughout Javanese history (and throughout the history of all Malay peoples) in the *kris*, a dagger-like weapon. Since it was both a package of power and a symbol of power, its maker was a man of some consequence. The *kris* makers of old were thought to be able to forge the metal with the heat from their thumbs.

The preservation of caste was one role for centuries of the art of batik making. The Javanese aristocracy, the *priyayi*, reserved for themselves the designing and drawing, as well as the wearing, of certain patterns. At the top of the list were mystically powerful patterns reserved, as they still are, for the sultan of Jogjakarta and his family.

Between the fall of the second kingdom of Mataram and the establishment of independence Javanese attitudes were to some extent affected by the rule of the Dutch. Understandably, former colonies are always rather touchy about the extent of the influence their colonial masters had on them. In Indonesia's case the question is complicated by the fact that the Dutch colonial rulers entirely lacked flamboyance, or even style. They were in Indonesia for 350 years. The Dutch economy depended enormously on the East Indies, and so did Dutch self-esteem. It made them, after all, an imperial power in the days when those words could still be used in polite society. But their role remains rather enigmatic.

The Dutch language is not a lingua franca as English, French, Spanish, or Portuguese are elsewhere. Indonesians were not encouraged to learn it and Indonesian elite groups did not copy Dutch manners. The Dutch made no great missionary effort. Sizeable Christian groups in north-central Sumatra and in some of the smaller eastern islands are the fruits of German and Portuguese missionary activity. The Dutch hardly disturbed the ancient system of *adat*, or customary law. They ruled, and counted the money.

But if there was no romance about the Dutch presence, it did leave its mark. In some old buildings and town plans, of course—but most important, in the minds of those who would later rule Indonesia.

62, 63. A batik factory in Jogjakarta where the women earn the equivalent of about one dollar a day. They are tracing the various designs in hot wax.

64. Tiled roofs and a paved square are reminders of Dutch colonial days in the older part of Jakarta.

Dutch education for the chosen few was the conduit through which squeezed the last pieces to make up the intellectual and cultural mosaic of twentieth-century Indonesia—the values and social theories of the West.

When Dutch ships began sniffing around the Indonesian islands at the end of the sixteenth century they found prosperous agricultural communities, flourishing trade between the islands, and several ports full of ships from as far north as China and as far west as Turkey. They founded the city of Batavia, which is now Jakarta, in 1619. For all that century the United Dutch East India Company fought off attacks everywhere in the islands. Already they were using mercenaries from one island to fight in another. Gradually they extended a sort of rule over most of the islands. They took over all significant inter-island trade. They imposed systems of agricultural tribute which provided them with a profitable flow of spices, tobacco, copra, and coffee. Like the English colonists elsewhere, they divided and ruled. They reached agreements with the princes of western Java, turned them into regents, and ruled through them. They took over the existing bureaucracy of the Javanese sultanates.

In southern Sumatra the Dutch imported thousands of Chinese in the nineteenth century to work sugar and tobacco plantations. In Java, Chinese settlement had been going on peaceably enough for centuries, and many Chinese were prosperous merchants. Like the Indonesians later, the Dutch discriminated against the Chinese, refusing them equality under the law and restricting their right to travel. None the less they found the Chinese very useful as economic middlemen and, most notoriously, as tax farmers. Under this system Javanese sultans made over estates to Chinese tax farmers, who then had two obligations. One was to pay rent to the sultan, and the other to pay taxes to the Dutch. Whatever they could wring out of the local people in addition to that, they kept for themselves. Indonesian resentment of the Chinese continues today.

Dr. Mely Tan, Jakarta sociologist:

The major source of friction as I see it is that Indonesians look at the Chinese minority as a group that is over-represented in the economy. They have a dominant role in the economy, and this has its roots in the colonial policy which found it profitable and useful to give them that role. Since independence, and even before then, Indonesian entrepreneurs have been trying to change this situation and the government has backed these efforts. What Indonesians want now is to have more representative participation of ethnic Indonesians in the economy. These efforts continue, and have even been getting stronger in recent years. Some critics feel that because Indonesia is opening up its economy to foreign investment and foreign capital, these efforts are somewhat frustrated because of the tendency of foreign enterprises to look for partners from among the more enterprising and financially stronger ethnic Chinese entrepreneurs.

65. Rice terraces in the hill north of Denpasar, Bali.

In a society with at least three levels of exploitation of the ordinary people—one by their own rulers, a second by foreign tax farmers, and a third by the colonial power—corruption is certain to flourish. It did, and despite the changed circumstances of independence, it still does. Student groups, some of the military people, and intellectuals familiar with modern ethics of public service, all condemn corruption from time to time. There have been official enquiries into it. It continues, as it does in almost all Asian countries and in not a few elsewhere. People in high and lowly positions of authority are not well paid, officially, but many of them take the opportunity to increase their income by demanding a rake-off for performing tasks which are part of their normal work, such as issuing licences. They usually keep only part of the money themselves, passing some of it on to their subordinates. The system is very old and well understood, and in a sense it works smoothly. But it extends to high levels and means that money intended to help the people, including some foreign aid, is heavily milked on the way down.

The system is consistent with the Javanese idea of power. It is difficult to establish a public service ethic in a bureaucracy which sees itself as being responsible solely to the central source of power and not to the people or to some abstraction called "the public interest". In any case, what modern moralists might call corruption—the feathering of bureaucratic nests—might have seemed no more than prudent insurance to the Dutch, who were frequently hard pressed until the beginning of this century to keep the peace and keep the profits flowing. There were constant revolts against colonial rule, some of them very serious, like the one led by the Javanese hero Prince Diponegoro in the late 1820s. Eventually the Dutch extended their occupation to most of the Indonesian islands. One of the last to fall was Bali.

66. A Balinese temple dancer performs for tourists.

The Balinese fascinate their fellow Indonesians as they fascinate Western visitors. To the stern Muslim from Aceh there is something rather shocking about the sensual grace of their dances, and their infidel ceremonies. To the businessman from Java, Bali is a place to refresh the spirit as it is for businessmen from Sydney, San Francisco, and Frankfurt. In a nation of cultural diversity Bali is more diverse than anywhere.

The religion of Bali is its own distinctive blend of local animism, ancestor-worship, and Hinduism. The Hindu belief was brought to Bali by priestly refugees from Java fleeing the advance of Islam in the middle ages. A modified version of the Hindu caste system took hold. The full names of Balinese even today include a name appropriate to their caste. They worship one god, but in various manifestations, including the Hindu trinity of Vishnu, Brahma, and Siva, who share the pantheon with a multitude of spirits. There is a dark side, too. The Balinese have an extensive demonology. Gods and spirits in Bali are familiar, everyday things. They are lived with in close relationship, their shrines in the gardens of homes, offices, and hotels are provided with food, thanks, propitiation, or whatever seems appropriate.

67. Food prepared for a ceremony at a Hindu temple, Bali (below).

68. A Hindu funeral pyre, Bali.

Words like "alienation", and similar terror-symbols from the mythologies of the West, still have no meaning for most Balinese. The basis of their society has been the integration of man, his family, his faith, and his art. Until the middle of this century, when Westerners arrived in numbers, the Balinese had no concept of art as an enterprise in its own right. Drawing, painting, carving, dancing were just things which almost everyone did, as part of life. It is a kind of in-nocence which cannot survive—in fact has not survived. Statues of gods and demons and carvings and paintings in a degenerate "Balinese style" are in mass production now in open-fronted workshops along the main tourist roads. It is almost an axiom of tourist development that it destroys what it comes to enjoy.

The first European to visit Bali was Captain de Houtman, the Dutchman who was later killed in Aceh. He landed in 1597 to a warm welcome and sailed for home some months later without half his crew, who refused to leave. A friendly relationship between the Dutch and the Balinese continued for some time. Eventually, however, it dawned on the Balinese that there was more to it than doing a bit of trade with the large, pale, and predatory foreigners. They resisted closer involvement, and in particular they resisted Dutch control and occupation. At the end of last century the Balinese royal families fought a war of extraordinary tenacity against the Dutch. The Dutch won, of course, being armed with modern weapons, although it took them a long time to do it. They destroyed the courtly structure at the top of Balinese society. But this was not until 1906 and by then it was, in a way, already too late. Dutch control of In-donesia was complete—and doomed. Almost at the moment of the fall of Bali, Indonesian nationalism found its voice.

It all began peaceably enough. The honour of being first in the field belongs to education, around which the first nationalist group was organized. It was called Budi Utomo, or "high endeavour", and was formed in 1908 to stimulate a sense of national dignity through education. It was an elite group and never had a mass following, but it began the important connection between education—particularly the student body—and the nationalist movement. Several times stu-dents have turned out as the catalyst, or even the moving force, in political situations both before and after independence. The first true mass movement for nationalism was Sarekat Islam, or Islamic As-sociation, which began in 1909 as a trading society to protect Indone-sians from Chinese dealers and grew from there, until it split even-tually into communist and moderate wings.

69. A young Balinese sculptor caters for the tourist trade (far left).
70. A Hindu temple, Bali.

The idea of unity and ambition for nationhood gathered emotional force for forty years. Nationalist leaders were banished or imprisoned, and nationalist movements were suppressed energetically by the

Dutch. Japanese occupation from 1942 to 1945 showed how brittle were the European claims to superiority. The Japanese have even more difficulty than Westerners do in understanding other Asian societies. They threw away any chance they had for long-term friendship and cooperation with the Indonesian people by the brutal pursuit of short-term goals, such as sending forced labour gangs to the Asian mainland. But they did help the nationalist movement, intentionally and otherwise. They ruled through Indonesian bureaucrats as the Dutch had done, but they allowed the Indonesians to gain much wider experience. They trained hundreds of Indonesians as army officers. They encouraged the use of Bahasa Indonesia, a form of Malay, as the national language (although apparently they intended that Japanese should eventually be the lingua franca or at least the language of government, since they began its compulsory teaching in schools).

The declaration of independence in 1945 was followed by four years of savage fighting against the returning Dutch, and briefly against a British force, interspersed with negotiations at the United Nations and elsewhere.

The first president, Sukarno, assumed leadership of a nation whose cultural diversity and regional loyalties were overridden only temporarily by nationalist emotion. Around him were men representing a wide range of beliefs and ambitions. There were Dutch-educated members of the Indonesian elite group familiar with, and variously committed to, European ideas of socialism or capitalism. There were Communist Party members, overt and otherwise. There were conservative Muslims, and others influenced by modern, Middle Eastern Islamic scholarship. There were professional soldiers who saw themselves, familiarly in the history of the Third World, as a modernizing and unifying elite.

Under President Sukarno Indonesia tried first of all a liberal parliamentary democracy on the European model, then a mixture of local and imported ideas called Guided Democracy. Sukarno himself was a Javanese firmly within the Javanese tradition. Power was concentrated in him personally. He drew power from the people—not in the modern (or Minangkabau) sense of gaining their consent, although he certainly had that for some time, but in a magical sense of drawing power from their physical presence at mass rallies. Sukarno was a seductive orator who spoke in apocalyptic terms about his "global strategy", and whose vision embraced a role of world importance for himself and for Indonesia. His way of leading the people forward, however, was to look backward. He appealed constantly to the glories of the Majapahit empire. His speeches were thick with inspirational references to the virtues of traditional village life in Java,

71. Jakarta's national mosque, planned originally by Sukarno to be the biggest in the world. The slender tower and domed building are part of the same enormous complex.

with its cooperative spirit. It was a highly romantic and idealized version of traditional life, but it was a way of capturing the imagination of the ordinary people—especially when Sukarno himself played to the hilt the role of one of the most appealing figures in Javanese mythology: the Just Prince, a messiah.

National politics since Sukarno have been in a lower key, but enough of the style remains to be galling to Indonesians more imbued with modern political concepts and less impressed by Javanese mysticism.

The forces for unity in modern Indonesia are various, and powerful. One of them is education, at least at lower levels. Indonesian society impresses its norms and values on children's minds as all societies do. The national education system is trying to establish the heroes of early times as national, rather than regional, figures.

Indonesia is very alive to the influence of the mass media as a force for unity. The police produce a weekly series of television situation comedies, using actors who are also members of the national police force, to spread the law and order message in a palatable way and to improve the force's relationship with the public. The army also produces television programmes with similar aims.

Some uses of the media edge towards conformity rather than unity. Official news is provided for television and radio broadcasts. Newspapers are censored with a fluctuating degree of severity. Some have been closed down, and journalists detained.

72. A street scene in Surabaya, eastern Java.

In rural areas the radio is particularly important. The government radio service uses the national language to draw even remote areas into a sense of belonging, as well as to serve more practical educational purposes with talks for farmers on technical and marketing matters.

It is no use telling people they are one nation if they do not feel like one. What people feel, even if they are not articulate about it, is to be seen in their art. Indonesia's artistic expression is still highly diverse, which is both a richness and an embarrassment. Other islanders believe that overcrowded, underfed Java hogs the artistic limelight as it does the national economy. Some artists are themselves trying to find a way to unity in art. Perhaps the best known is the choreographer and batik painter Bagong Kussudiardja, of Jogjakarta.

Bagong Kussudiardja:
I teach the basics of traditional Javanese dance and now also a new thing—I teach the basics of the traditional dances that I know from other parts of Indonesia and also modern ballet technique from Europe and America. I marry all these techniques. The dances I have created in this fashion are in a universal language and can be understood anywhere through the beauty of sound and movement. I am an Indonesian citizen in the field of art. I want to create an Indonesian art, a national art that can represent all Indonesia, not just Java, or Bali, or wherever.

Bagong is a Christian—but a Javanese Christian, as is obvious in his batik painting of a crucifixion. The idea of a messiah is well within his own cultural tradition, but he is not moved by Christ the pale Galilean, the sacrifice. Bagong's Christ has the face of a *wayang* puppet—the aquiline profile of a Hindu god-king. What Java needs in its Christ is the hero, the possessor of power.

In the last resort, temporal power belongs to the ones who have the guns. The Indonesian armed forces have the power to coerce, and from time to time they have used it. There are still political prisoners and detainees, perhaps as many as thirty thousand. Repression is not obvious to the visitor or, apparently, particularly brutal. But the imposed discipline is there.

The armed forces are playing down their military strength and emphasizing their role as citizens, as a *cooperating* force for unity. Military officers have replaced, or work alongside, civilian officials at all levels down to the village. Officers are to be found as university professors, doctors, business executives. Less exalted ranks are frequently to be found building country roads or in the fields, showing the villagers that even though they are soldiers they are workers too. This idea is being pushed enthusiastically now, but it is not a new one.

Brigadier-general Nugroho Notosusanto:

> At one stage of the war of independence the Indonesians had to adopt guerilla tactics because of the superiority in arms of the enemy, and during this guerilla period the armed forces were completely integrated with the people. The soldiers not only performed the military function, they also performed a social function, helping the people in their fields, caring for the health of the people, building houses, and so on. This tradition was continued after the war of independence when the Republic entered a period of internal upheaval, when national unity was threatened by forces from the left and from the right. The armed forces again not only performed a military function, trying to suppress the rebellions, but also helped people to rebuild villages, bridges, roads, and mosques.

The armed forces, working now for national unity, have not always been united themselves. Regional loyalties and modern ideologies have divided them in more than one violent uprising, but most notably at the time of the attempted leftist and communist coup in 1965 which effectively ended the Sukarno era. Shock troops kidnapped six generals and stuffed their bodies down a well called the Crocodile Hole, just outside Jakarta.

In the weeks following, Indonesia suffered a terrible paroxysm of violence as troops and civilians alike set about annihilating the Communist Party. No one knows how many other scores were settled, or exactly how many died. It may well have been between three hundred thousand and half a million.

What the mass slaughter says about the darker recesses of the Indonesian race memory is, perhaps, not for a stranger to judge. But it is clear that the cultural diversity a visitor is able to see, or to capture on film, is only symbolic of deeper currents. Indonesia, in fact, is more than most a nation of symbols. From Borobudur to Balinese dances to *kris* makers to the phallic, flame-topped monument in modern Jakarta, ancient symbols are still recognized, still powerful. But not all-powerful, as Sukarno thought they were.

The events of 1965 were part of the price Indonesia paid for yielding to the peculiar seduction of the nation's cultural heritage, and especially that of Java. The temptation of Borobudur's quietude, the obsessional style of the Javanese aristocrat, the mystic power of the puppet-master, is to believe that form is more important than content, that the symbol will serve for the fact. It will not, and Indonesians have now reminded themselves of that in a very Indonesian way by building a dramatic monument at the Crocodile Hole.

As a symbol.

4 Malaysia

Sparrow with Sparrow, Raven with Raven
(Malay proverb: *Pipit sama pipit, enggang sama enggang*)

Malaysia is the only Southeast Asian country in which Islam is the official, state religion. That is one of two crucial facts about the nation. The other is its racial balance; and "balance" is almost the precise word. Malaysia is the only Asian country—one of very few countries anywhere, surely—in which no one race has an overwhelming majority of the population. Just over half the twelve million Malaysians are Malays; not much short of 40 per cent are Chinese; the rest are mainly Indians, with some Pakistanis, other Asians, Eurasians, and Europeans. Such a mixture is volatile. The Malaysians know that, and have the scars to prove it. So far they have not found the answer to racial sensitivity, but they are trying.

More than 60 per cent of the Malay people live in rural areas. For them the centre of life is the village, and the centre of village life is the mosque. Islam permeates every aspect of life at the grass roots level. The pace of life is much the same as it always was—slow, tied to the seasons. But expectations rise, and perspectives change. The growth of political life since independence has meant some loss of influence for the traditional informal leadership of age, piety, and wisdom. There is still respect for men who wear the white cap of the *haji*—denoting those who have made the pilgrimage to Mecca—but even in religious leadership there is change. The *imam*, the religious leader of the village, is now a paid official of the state. The bureaucrats, who are inheriting the earth everywhere, have inherited the road to heaven as well in Malaysia.

Amid the changes in Malay village life, and despite the creeping takeover by Japanese motorbikes and blue jeans, there is one constant. The view from down there has not changed; it is still a view of society from the bottom of the heap. Almost everyone is better off than the rural Malays. In particular, and most obviously, the Chinese are better off. There are poor Chinese, but not many. Even the rural Chinese have an average income twice that of the rural Malays.

Since independence the Malays have been asking themselves some questions about this—about how the Malays came to be the poorest group in their own country. Everyone knows that it came about large-

73. A Malay boy in a Trengganu village.

74. The pace of communication in traditional Malay villages has increased somewhat with the advent of the ubiquitous Japanese motorcycle.
75. The remains of an Indian temple in the northern Malay state of Kedah, on the west coast of the peninsula (below opposite).

76, 77. The sultan and sultana of Kedah at a ceremony to mark their return home after serving a five-year term as king and queen of Malaysia (below).

ly during British control of the country. This leads some politicians and others to say that it is all the fault of the British. But is it? Could the fact that Malays have not so far managed to compete economically against the Chinese, and to a lesser extent against the Indians, have something to do with the Malays' own attitudes and values? With Islam, perhaps? Is there something in their culture and religion which is a handicap to what modern societies call progress? The answers lie scattered through the nation's history.

The Malay people came down the peninsula in waves from Yunnan, south China, beginning about 2500 B.C. The last wave, only about nine hundred years ago, was really a backwash of Malay immigration from the islands of Java and Sumatra. There were wealthy settlements on the west coast of the Malay peninsula many hundreds of years ago. Their people were Malay, their culture was to some extent Indian. This was the result of influence by Indian traders. From the fourth century northern Malaya became one of a string of Indian-style kingdoms. Others appeared in what are now Indonesia, Thailand, and the Khmer republic. Archeologists have found near the coast of the northern state of Kedah the remains of Indian temples and relics of buildings which suggest sizeable trading towns. The Indian influence was first felt, and then transmitted downwards, by the royal courts.

The sultans' courts of the Malay states continued for centuries to act as a channel and filter for outside influence. For example, when the sultan of Kedah returned recently to his capital, Alor Star, after a

five-year term as the national monarch, he did so with the kind of parade-ground ceremony familiar to any Englishman. The uniforms, the drill on parade, were British. So was the inscrutable habit, evident in the official guests' enclosure, of wearing suits and ties in tropical climates.

The borrowings by the royal courts have not been haphazard. The practices, styles, and beliefs adopted by the Malay courts through the centuries have been ones which were more efficient or more convincing than the old ones, which were to the advantage of the ruling elite, or which seemed likely to buttress the legitimacy of the court itself. The courts became Buddhist, Hindu, and finally Muslim. Hindu idols and temples were destroyed, being too direct an offence against Islam's prohibition on representations of the human body. But on the whole the version of Islam which came filtered through India was a tolerant one. Rajas became sultans, many gods became one, and slowly the ordinary people followed the lead of the court. Traditions which had woven themselves into the fabric of court ceremonial were left undisturbed; one important example of this is the sacred, originally Hindu *nobat* orchestra which in some states still plays for royal occasions, and which confers magical powers on the sultan by drumming him in at his coronation.

Conversion to Islam was painless, but slow. A more dramatic expansion of the faith, and of the importance of the Malay peninsula, had to await the conversion to Islam in the fifteenth century of the trading state of Malacca.

Malacca became important first of all because of where it is, and the way the winds blow. Long before the Christian era Indian sailors were riding the southwest monsoon in search of cloves, pepper, and sandalwood. Chinese junks followed the northeast monsoon over the China sea, bringing silk and porcelain to trade for gold and spices. Halfway point, where the monsoons, the tides, and the ships all met, was in the Straits of Malacca. In early centuries pirates from Malacca preyed savagely on passing ships. They became so notorious that traders from India put their goods ashore at their new settlement in Kedah and carried them across the peninsula to be picked up again on the east coast. There was a flourishing connection for a time between the east coast and Annam, now part of central Vietnam.

By the 1400s Malacca had become rich, respectable, and Muslim. Much of the Islamic influence came in from Aceh, the first Indonesian state to embrace the faith, just across the straits in northern Sumatra. By the end of the fifteenth century Malacca had prospered so much that its influence spread over much of the Malay peninsula and over large areas of Sumatra as well. Malacca was briefly the most important trading empire in southeastern Asia. Flattering visits were

78. View of a Malacca street from the tower of a mosque.

paid by the Chinese eunuch admiral, Cheng Ho. A temple in Malacca is dedicated to him. China at this time was vigorous and enquiring, and blandly sure of its own importance. A ruler of Malacca visited China to pay prudent tribute to the emperor.

Muslim Malays and Indians provided the Malacca ruling elite. Chinese settlers provided much of the entrepreneurial flair. Javanese mercenary soldiers provided the security, or so they thought. This was the high point of what is regarded now as classical Malay culture. There was money, leisure, and a sophisticated elite to encourage all the arts. The version of Islam adopted and promoted by Malacca was Sufism, an Indian variant with a heavy infusion of mysticism. This is the period Malays think of when they confront the European-centred view of history which assumes that nothing of any interest happened in the area until the white man arrived. In fact, the first age of wealth and culture was not begun, but ended, by the coming of the Europeans.

The Portuguese conquered Malacca in 1511 and built a fortress. They held Malacca for more than a hundred years, and ruled as the Portuguese usually did—with a fair degree of racial tolerance and an extreme degree of brutality and pious tyranny. Their descendants still carry such names as da Silva, d'Souza, Dias, and Pinto, in the Eurasian communities of Malaysia and Singapore. A group of about five hundred lives in Malacca, a close little community clinging to its sense of difference. It has lost advantages in employment in official enterprises, such as the railways, which it held under British rule. The community is still served by the Catholic church, which has never gained more than a toehold on the Malay peninsula, being identified not just with Europeans but with violence and conquest.

The Dutch captured Malacca in 1641 and held it for a hundred and eighty years—leaving behind, typically, an administration building. The British took over Malacca in 1824, in exchange for which the Dutch received a small British settlement in Sumatra called Bencoolen. It was part of a deal by which these two small and faraway European countries divided between them control of the whole world of the Malays. It was also to pacify the Dutch for a bit of sharp practice by the governor of Bencoolen, who had just bought the island of Singapore. His name was Thomas Stamford Raffles.

Despite their fine buildings, their even finer pretensions, and their undeniable power, it was not the Europeans who left the deepest mark on Malacca. The city today, like most in Malaysia, is overwhelmingly Chinese. Some are descendants of the very early settlers, known later as Baba Chinese, who adopted Malay language and dress and who perhaps represent what might have been if Chinese immigration had remained gradual. Most of Malacca's Chinese now

are descendants of the thousands who flooded in during the nineteenth century. They were attracted first by the booming economies of the three British-owned cities known as the Straits settlements—Singapore, Malacca, and Penang. Then thousands more came to work in tin mines owned largely, at that time, by the rulers of the Malay states. The Chinese arrived mainly through Singapore. Most of them moved up the peninsula or stayed inside Singapore. Some crossed to Sumatra to work for the Dutch. A few went the other way, to the small, rather mysterious settlements on the huge island of Borneo.

The Malaysian Borneo states of Sabah and Sarawak share borders with the Indonesian province of Kalimantan. They have a colourful and violent history of piracy and headhunting. Both these proclivities were brought more or less under control last century.

In Sarawak the Englishman James Brooke became the first white raja, imposing law and order with the occasional help of the Royal Navy and resisting outside influence or even investment, in the interests of his people, as he saw it. Sabah was run as a commercial enterprise by the North Borneo Chartered Company until World War II, and afterwards became a development responsibility of the British government. Sabah and Sarawak chose to join the Federation of Malaysia in 1963.

Chinese dominate the cities of the Borneo states, but this similarity to peninsular Malaysia is misleading. For one thing, there are more rural Chinese in Borneo. Politics are not organized so closely along racial lines as they are on the peninsula. Sabah and Sarawak do not have a Muslim, or a Malay, majority. The Malays are outnumbered by the local ethnic groups and the Chinese together. The people in Sabah especially have ethnic and historical links with the people of the Sulu sultanate in the southern Philippines.

Sabah and Sarawak are both keenly jealous of their states' rights within the federal system, and have occasionally insisted on their own way, to the embarrassment of Kuala Lumpur. They provide Malaysia's only important example of a problem which plagues neighbouring Indonesia—the pressure of regionalism against rule from the centre.

The Indians were the last of the three major groups to arrive on the Malay peninsula. The ones here now have nothing to do with the Indians who brought Islam to Malaya many centuries ago. The descendants of some were brought out by the British as soldiers, policemen, and minor functionaries during the heyday of the Straits settlements in the middle of last century. Most arrived at the start of this century for the specific purpose of growing rubber.

The local Malays showed little interest in plantation work,

82. Detail of the decoration inside an Indian Hindu temple at Batu caves, near Kuala Lumpur.

83. An Indian rubber-tapper at work in Selangor state.

presumably because they had an adequate subsistence from their village land and from fishing. The Chinese were sometimes difficult to control. The main reason for importing most of the plantation labour from southern India, however, was that the first plantation owners and managers came from there and from Ceylon, and preferred the workers they were used to. The estate workers came to Malaya on contracts, with the intention of returning to India when they had made enough money. Very many of them did. However enough remained over the years to ensure a permanent Indian community. Nowadays the Indian workers on some of the more decrepit plantations provide the only group which might challenge the poorest rural Malaya as the most wretched part of Malaysian society. A number of Indians are wealthy either through commerce or as members of the professions. Even more are moderately prosperous shopkeepers or small traders. Most of the Indians are Hindus, although there are some Sikhs and some Muslims.

Even such a bald and potted account of the background of the three major ethnic groups in Malaysia suggests the artificiality of the situation in which they found themselves at the time of independence in 1957. Their circumstances had all in various ways been arranged, or at any rate influenced, to suit the interests of yet another party, the British. Now they were left to build a nation together and to compete, as part of that task, for economic and political power.

Some Malays themselves have argued that some doctrines of Islam have held Malays back in economic competition. Certainly Islam has

86. Girl at a Koran class in Trengganu. Islam dominates every aspect of life in traditional Malay villages.

been a strong influence on the Malays for centuries. The present constitution of Malaysia, in fact, includes the profession of the Islamic faith as one of the things which determine who is a Malay. Islam does forbid Muslims to lend money at interest, which on the face of it is a handicap to business life in a capitalist system. However, more generous interpretations of doctrine are possible. Straightforward usury is certainly forbidden to Muslims (therefore effectively reserving the money-lending business for Chinese and non-Muslim Indians.) But it is possible, for instance, for the Malaysian government to run an investment fund to send people to Mecca on the pilgrimage. The results of investment in the fund are not called interest, but profit, and there is no doctrinal objection to making a reasonable profit. Islam regards thrift and conscientious work as virtues. The history of Islam internationally includes many instances of energetic and adventurous trading—which is, indeed, the reason for Islam's coming to Malaya in the first place. So far as the competitive society goes, there is nothing essential to Islamic doctrine which would prevent a Malay from succeeding in business.

Some thoughtful Malays are convinced that the most important reason for the Malays' position is simple the force of historical and cultural circumstance.

87. Mosque in Kuala Trengganu, the capital of the east coast state of Trengganu.

Tunku Abdul Rahman, former Malaysian Prime Minister:

The British, when they took over this country, thought of only one thing, that is to exploit all the wealth that this country has. So they brought people from China, from India—countries with millions upon millions of population who have to struggle, to steal, in order to live in their own country. And when you brought those people and forced them on to us, people who like to take things easy, how in the world can we compete against them? Apart from everything else, they had had all the experiences in their own country, as I say, they had to struggle, they had to learn, they had to work the hard way. It's just impossible; we were never given much chance.

Life in a Malay village is not terribly challenging, on the face of it. The villagers depend on co-operative work in fishing or agriculture. Certainly the farmers and fishermen work very hard when necessary, as anyone must whose living has to obey the rhythms of tides and seasons, but they seem not to be burdened by the impulse to sustained effort which drives some other races, notably the Chinese.

88. Tunku Abdul Rahman, former prime minister of Malaysia, at his home in Penang.

89—94. The different aspects of village life in Trengganu state: dressed in a sarong of vibrant Malaysian batik, a villager splits coconut husks and a grandfather does his share of the childminding (above opposite); a musician plays his flute, and villagers winnow rice with the aid of a hand propellor (below opposite); graceful fishing boats wait by the shore (above); and a young woman does the washing (right).

The basic unit of the Malay village is the nuclear family, but regular contact with grandparents and other relations is easy. The whole village may be loosely bound by ties of kinship. The village tends to regard formality highly, and to equate what is traditional with what is good. Old country pastimes and habits of mind are persistent. Despite changes and outside pressures, the influence of Malay village life is still conservative. The Malays have always been used to a hierarchy of rank and privilege, with the sultans' courts at the top. The British habit of ruling through a local upper class made it easy for Malays to transfer respect to government officials.

The British even started a copy of the English public school to turn the sons of the Malay nobility into administrators with a sense of noblesse oblige. Malay College, Kuala Kangsar, still performs much the same function today, although some boys from all social backgrounds are admitted on merit.

95. Boys relaxing in the grounds of Malay College, Kuala Kangsar, which is based on the English style public school.

The British and upper-class Malay styles coincided nicely. Malays fitted the higher reaches of administration as to the manor born. There is still some difficulty, even in schools less high-toned than Kuala Kangsar, in getting Malay students interested in science and technology. The British, and the Malays themselves after independence, were obliged to use Chinese as professional and technical officers. The flourishing of Chinese in these roles and as economic middlemen and entrepreneurs was due in some part to British policy, but even more to the Chinese own attitudes and values.

The world the Chinese are adapted to is urban, businesslike, crowded, noisy, and prosperous. It is possible to understand that the Chinese might cause offence, or at any rate provoke envy, among other groups. When they have money they do not mind it showing. To people whose tastes are more austere, maybe through necessity, the Chinese exuberance of style may be taken as vulgarity. A bit of

96. Encrusted with decoration is this Khoo Kongsi clan association house in Penang.

swank is understandable. Chinese success in Malaysia is something to show off about. It is not haphazard. Inside a free enterprise, capitalist system the Chinese have played their own system, like Chinese minorities everywhere. It is a system based on the rural verities of old China: in some ways similar to those of old Malaya, in other ways very different. Respect for age is there, and respect for learning—but in the Chinese case it is respect for secular learning. The Confucian tradition is not theological. Family ties are there too, but more extensive and exclusive than for the Malays.

One of the most striking monuments in Asia to the Chinese system is the elaborately decorated Khoo Kongsi clan association house in Penang. Clan associations were set up to help new arrivals from China in the early days with jobs, money (on loan) to make a start, and welfare when things went wrong. The clan associations and extended family tradition together encouraged relationships of trust in business. By its nature, the system is exclusive. People who are not Chinese simply cannot belong to it. So many enterprises, including very large ones, are based on Chinese family and clan connections that the Malays feel, and are, shut out.

The Chinese community enjoys noisy and colourful festivals. For that matter, the festivals provide a good deal of enjoyment for the other communities, too. One of the best known is the moon festival, held on the fifteenth day of the eighth moon. This probably began centuries ago in some kind of harvest festival, but it has acquired a confused mythology in which the moon is populated by a three-legged toad, an old man who prepares marriages, and a rabbit which makes moon cakes (small round pastry envelopes filled with a sweet-piquant mixture of fruits and spices).

In the fourteenth century the people of southern China rebelled against the Mongols of Kublai Khan. The revolt was led by Buddhist monks and members of secret societies. The signal to begin was given on the night of the moon festival, so it is said, written on slips of paper hidden in moon cakes. The highly popular festival thus celebrates, ironically, one of the things least popular about the Chinese—a taste for clannish secrecy, a reputation for deviousness.

The early Chinese arrivals in Malaya brought their secret societies with them. There were some fierce gang wars—some of them so bloody, in fact, that they prompted the British to intervene in Malay states which they had not intended to take over. Or so they said. The Chinese are not the only ones with a reputation for deviousness.

The Malaysian Chinese, at any rate, see nothing mysterious about their success in economic competition.

Mr. Lim Heng Kiap, Selangor State MP:

Most of the Malaysian Chinese are from the provinces of Canton and Hok-kien. They are very hilly provinces and the soil is not so fertile. I think that was the main reason why the Chinese people from the two provinces were prompted to come to Malaysia to seek a livelihood. I think that's a great challenge. Another thing I would like to emphasize is the spirit of unity. This is quite basic in the Chinese culture, the community feeling. When they came here they still kept themselves together, as you can see. When they are eating, for instance, they sit around a round table, they use chopsticks and they pick from the same plates. It's the culture of unity that basically counts for the success of the Malaysian Chinese.

Malays are suspicious of the interest some local Chinese have always shown in ideology and in the affairs of mother China. In the early 1900s money from the comparatively wealthy immigrants helped to finance the revolts organized by Dr. Sun Yat Sen which eventually overthrew the Manchu dynasty and began the Chinese Republic. Dr. Sun himself spent some time in Singapore and Malaya. Many Malayan Chinese joined overseas branches of the Kuomintang, the Chinese nationalist organization. Chinese schools were set up in the peninsula and in Singapore, producing a group of nationalist-inclined Chinese whose interests did not coincide with those of the increasing number of English-educated Chinese born in the Straits settlements of Singapore, Malacca, and Penang.

Despite the Chinese "culture of unity" the plural society being created in Malaya thus included (and still includes, to a reducing extent) division among the Chinese community. This was increased in the 1930s when communism began to compete with the Kuomintang for Chinese support.

During World War II the Communist Party provided, as it did elsewhere, a main prop of anti-Japanese resistance. In the twelve-year emergency beginning in 1948 the Malayan Communist Party waged guerilla war first against the British and then, after 1957, against the new independent government. Most of the guerillas were Chinese. At the time of independence the British had to redraft their plans to hand over government, because the Malays feared the Chinese would have too much power.

Singapore, overwhelmingly Chinese, joined Malaya, Sabah, and Sarawak in the new Federation of Malaysia in 1963. After two years Singapore was asked to leave the federation, and did so, largely because of racial tensions and because the Malays had been alarmed by the signs of Singaporean (and therefore Chinese) political activity creeping up the Malay peninsula.

Out of all this recent history some practical policies have sprung. The Malaysian government decided that Malays would not be able to climb up from the bottom of the economic heap unless they were given some help. So there is an extensive policy to promote Malay interests in various fields—land ownership, education, loan funds, and so on. Malays have certain preferences in governmental employment. There is a plan to increase Malay ownership in business enterprises from 3 per cent to 30 per cent in thirty years. That is an attempt to create in one generation a whole middle class of entrepreneurs, by government policy. It's a fascinating experiment, but not without problems.

In 1971 the government passed a constitutional amendment to prevent public debate (even in parliament) of "sensitive issues" like this special position of the Malays. There are other signs of anxiety. Security surveillance of people with radical views is said to be quite strict, and there are people under detention.

There is a long history of Malay resentment of Chinese economic strength in the society, and a long history of Chinese resentment of Malay ruling prerogatives. It would be wrong, however, to think that there was a great gulf fixed between Malay and Chinese and that it could never be bridged. Towards the top of the social ladder the interests of all the racial groups are more likely to coincide. Successful men have an interest in maintaining the system within which they have risen to status, or been born to it. The higher levels of the Malay, Chinese, and Indian political groups cooperate fairly smoothly. At

these levels personal friendships between members of the different groups are not rare. The difficulty is to bring any warmth into relationships between the ordinary members of the different groups—or for that matter to encourage any relationships at all outside purely formal and necessary ones.

Professor Ungku Abdul Aziz, vice-chancellor, University of Malaya:

> I think one of the most important things is language. Malay is the national language, and we are using this as a teaching medium in primary schools and secondary schools, and introducing it into the university. Inside this country those who are going to be citizens should be able to communicate, that's the first requirement, absolutely basic I think. But then we all have our different cultures and these are very strong and very deep cultures, the Indian Hindu culture, the Chinese culture, the traditional beliefs, food, dress, ideas about heaven and hell and so on are all unique, and the music is very different. The only way we could have any unity is by learning to understand and appreciate each other's cultures. I don't think anybody should force each of the cultural groups into some kind of national sausage, this I think would be a terrible thing, but I think we could have a great thing going if we could learn really genuinely to appreciate each other's cultures.

For cultural and historical reasons ordinary Malays see the world arranged vertically. Relationships are understood in terms of higher and lower status. Authority, whether secular or religious, is accepted readily. The Chinese stereotype view is that the Malays are charming, lazy, and submissive. For the Chinese the important social relationships are horizontal, seen in terms of shared obligations to ancestors, kinfolk, and clan. Authority is accepted, of course, but it has no religious sanction. The Malay stereotype view is that the Chinese are clannish, grasping, and arrogant.

A television soap opera produced by the Malaysian government's film unit approaches obliquely the problems of building a multi-racial nation. It goes something like this:

*. Central Kuala Lumpur—style described by Dennis ͏oodworth as "late ͏ctorian Haroun-al-͏aschid".

Scenes	Plot line
Chinese man angrily admonishes daughter, wags finger, shakes head. Girl walks from house.	A Chinese girl is in trouble at home ...
Malay boy waits in park, girl walks up, they embrace, stroll off hand in hand.	... because she has a Malay boyfriend.
Young Chinese men lurk, looking stern. They leap into path of couple, attack boyfriend. In the melee one stabs the girl accidentally.	The girl's brother sets out to defend the family honour—with some help from his clumsy friends.
Ambulance sequence ... hospital sequence ... girl has transfusion of blood from boyfriend, lies in bed frail but appealing.	
Boyfriend stands by bed; girl's parents enter, hesitate, then greet him more or less warmly. Up music, fade image ...	The girl survives, her parents are reconciled with the Malay boyfriend, all seem set to live happily ever after.

But the ending of the film is a little vague. No one mentions a wedding. The film is not a plea for inter-racial marriage. Just real friendship, translated into community terms, would be triumph enough.

The most difficult part of all this is that cultural understanding and rapport, even if they are established, have to be translated eventually into political terms. Politics in Malaysia are organized along racial lines, and have been since long before independence. This has some disadvantages. It means that racial differences are formalized. It ensures that people see their social problems in racial terms.

An alternative, one which might relieve the pressure, would be to organize politics along the lines of different shared interests—a workers' party, a middle-class party maybe, the conservatives, the radicals, and so on; the way in which many Western societies have organized their political life for generations. That alternative, however, if the Malaysians were to adopt it, would raise the spectre of class conflict. It would put at risk the one firm thread running centrally through the culture of the Malay people—the sultanates, the royal courts, and the aristocratic tradition. That tradition, understandably enough, has no real emotional force for the Chinese people or for the other non-Malays.

The real Malaysian dilemma is not that one group is richer than another, or that one lot eats pork and the other doesn't—although of course these things are important and they are how people perceive the problem—but that no way has been found so far of casting political life in terms that are significant, meaningful, satisfying, for everybody.

5 The Philippines

The Furthest Cross

Among the many Asian nations which have emerged only recently from colonial rule, the Republic of the Philippines is the only one to have spent two significant periods under different colonial masters. Religion is a living force in many Asian societies, but only in the Philippines is that religion Christianity.

One might expect that a nation with that background would be one with a colourful character, and it is. But it can't make up its mind what that character is. The Filipinos are having identity trouble. The Philippines has been both a Spanish and an American colony. It is a product, someone has said, of three hundred years of the Inquisition and fifty years of Hollywood—enough to confuse anyone. Even independence since 1946 has not been smooth. Martial law was declared in 1972.

The concern with national identity however is not a hot topic of conversation in the villages. The people there know who they are. It is an elite group debate, but it affects everybody. This very division between the elite group and the rest, so familiar in developing countries, is in fact part of the problem. It began to emerge very soon after the first white men arrived in the Philippine islands and began to change the societies they found there.

A Spanish expedition led by the Portuguese navigator Ferdinand Magellan arrived in the Philippines in 1521, having rounded the tip of South America and crossed the Pacific—the first western route to the East Indies. The name still borne by the Philippines, after King Philip of Spain, is itself an echo of this first colonial adventure.

The Spanish were after three things. First, they wanted a share of the rich trade in spices, which were as necessary in European cooking then as they are now in most Asian cuisines. The big prize was the spice islands of the Moluccas, now part of Indonesia, but then a Portuguese monopoly. (The Spanish failed to break this monopoly.) Secondly, they sought a base for trade in China and Japan, an entrepot between the East and the colony in Mexico. And thirdly, as the foremost Christian nation in Europe, they wanted to carry the Cross to the East.

98. A charming building of the late Spanish period in a village on Cebu island.

At the township of Cebu in the central Philippines, the Spanish found a society with a complex structure of chiefs, aristocrats, free men, and slaves, a written but limited language, a code of law, and advanced forms of music and dancing. The local chief called himself a raja. The Spanish took this to mean that like a European king he held sway over the whole area. This was a mistake. The society was still fragmented, with local chiefs or datus acting independently and frequently in conflict. The rajas of Cebu and of Manila further north were in fact trying to extend their rule, and might have established sizeable kingdoms if the Spanish had not cut the process short. His misunderstanding of this state of affairs cost Magellan his life.

He called on all the local chiefs to swear allegiance to the raja of Cebu, who in turn became a vassal of the king of Spain. Lapu Lapu, the chief of a small island called Mactan, refused. Magellan tried to impose the raja's authority by force, and was killed in the battle. A rather dingy memorial stands near modern Cebu's airport on Mactan island. Magellan's exploits are memorialized on the back, opposite the door to the public convenience. The front is reserved for Lapu Lapu, who killed Magellan—and who is remembered now, with inspired hindsight, as the first Filipino to repel European aggression.

FERDINAND MAGELLAN'S DEATH

ON THIS SPOT FERDINAND MAGELLAN DIED ON APRIL 27, 1521, WOUNDED IN AN ENCOUNTER WITH THE SOLDIERS OF LAPULAPU, CHIEF OF MACTAN ISLAND. ONE OF MAGELLAN'S SHIPS, THE VICTORIA, UNDER THE COMMAND OF JUAN SEBASTIAN ELCANO, SAILED FROM CEBU ON MAY 1, 1521, AND ANCHORED AT SAN LUCAR DE BARRAMEDA ON SEPTEMBER 6, 1522, THUS COMPLETING THE FIRST CIRCUMNAVIGATION OF THE EARTH.

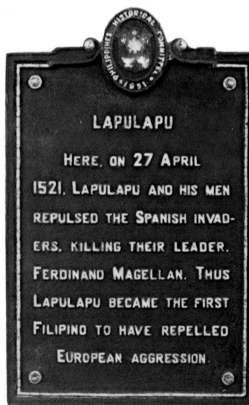

LAPULAPU

HERE, ON 27 APRIL 1521, LAPULAPU AND HIS MEN REPULSED THE SPANISH INVADERS, KILLING THEIR LEADER, FERDINAND MAGELLAN. THUS LAPULAPU BECAME THE FIRST FILIPINO TO HAVE REPELLED EUROPEAN AGGRESSION.

Although the elevation of Lapu Lapu as the first hero of Filipino nationalism is a common national trick—projecting the needs of modern societies on to their past, to make history useful—it is true that Cebu is crucial to the story of the Philippines. It is where the modern Philippines began, because it is where the Spanish landed. At Cebu the Filipinos first confronted not only the force but also the faith of the conquistadores. It is where Filipino Christianity began—and it began, in fact, with an odd little story.

After the death of Magellan several other expeditions set out from Mexico to the Philippine islands. None of them came to much, until 1565. In April that year a little fleet arrived off Cebu under the command of Miguel de Legazpi. The local people put up some resistance, and Legazpi bombarded the town. Then his men went ashore to see what they could find. One house was undamaged; inside it a sailor found what seemed to be a large doll, wrapped up, in a box. It was an image of the Holy Child Jesus—the Santo Nino.

The image had been given by Magellan to the wife of the raja of Cebu when she accepted baptism. Its discovery in the ruins forty-four years later was regarded as providential at the very least, and obviously called for some sort of religious celebration. It has been going on ever since. A large church, recently promoted to the status of a minor basilica, and a highly emotional cult, have grown around the small statue of the Santo Nino of Cebu.

99, 100. Memorials to the first circumnavigator of the earth, and the man who killed him (opposite).
101. The venerated statue of the Santo Nino in the minor basilica of Cebu city (right).

The Filipinos took to Christianity with dangerous fervour. It was easy to carry over into the church some of the magic and superstition of their folk religion based on rural animism. The Spanish friars were too few to be able to instruct all the converts sufficiently. Pagan worship of many idols and spirits became veneration, even worship, of many saints. Converts flocked to baptism when the idea got around that the sacrament not only washed away sin, but cured illnesses as well. Even today, among the less sophisticated, the church has not been able to disentangle relics of folk religion from Catholicism— especially rites to do with sickness and death. Village healers in the countryside near Cebu, for instance, still combine prayer and the laying on of hands with sharp puffs of breath to blow away evil spirits much older than Christianity.

In 1571 the Spanish moved their capital from Cebu to Manila, on Luzon island. A Muslim settlement ruled by Raja Soliman was captured, the raja was killed, and his small fortress on the Pasig River was replaced by a more imposing one named Fort Santiago. The fort and the walled settlement which grew up nearby were laid waste in World War II. Almost the only building remaining relatively intact today is the church of San Agustin.

With the move to Manila more Spanish friars arrived from Spain and Mexico. Most of the pacification of the Philippines was done by the Cross rather than the sword. There were very few large-scale military actions.

Father Horacio de la Costa, S.J.:

> The Catholic religion was brought to the Philippines by missionaries from Spain. They brought it to a people who were simply scattered tribes and clans in a collection of islands. What they did initially was to bring them to a further stage of economic and social organization by bringing them into towns and satellite villages under the bells of the parish church. By so doing they not only taught them the Christian religion but they also taught them the ways of settled agriculture and the ways of political life. They also, in the beginning, defended them from the exploitation of the conquistadores, and the first bishop of the Philippines, a Dominican, established that Filipinos could not be enslaved and that they should be taught in their own languages. In this way, through our own languages, the Christian religion has become a part of us. We have integrated it into the original basic religion that we had, of the gods of field and stream, and through the intercession of the saints and the rather flamboyant religious festivals that we have had we have become a Catholic people. Not only that, we have become a nation.

The church satisfied the Filipino taste for ritual, singing, and fiesta. The friars established their spiritual authority and had a good deal of temporal power as well. They founded hundreds of towns, started schools, built churches.

The churches of early colonial days show a taste for grandiose orna-

ment which the Filipinos have never lost. They show Chinese workmanship and even some Chinese decoration, because in the early days the Chinese were the only skilled artisans. The churches carry a certain echo of Mexican style, because after the first wave that was the way the Spanish influence arrived, filtered through their colonial experience in the Americas.

Intermarriage between Spaniards and local people—whom they called Indios after the Mexican manner—was not as frequent as in Mexico. One reason was the comparative rarity of Spaniards: there were never more than six thousand in the whole country. But there were plenty of informal liaisons by Filipinas with Spanish soldiers—and even, alas, with some friars who were lonely, a long way from home, and only human. Then, as now, the Filipinas were noted for their beauty.

One way and another there did emerge a class of mixed-race people who occupied a social position mid-way between the locals and the colonial masters. Filipinos were given Spanish names, but only the elite—the chiefs who became tax-gatherers and the children of an emerging, largely mixed-race land-owning class—were taught the Spanish language. Culturally the elite group was heavily influenced by Spain, although the ordinary people were less affected, except in the matter of religion.

There were in the sixteenth century, as there are now, people living in the mountains who were less advanced than those in the lowlands and coastal plains. An ethnologist's map of the Philippines is crowded and complicated, with something like three hundred groups and languages. For less scholarly purposes two main minority groupings may be useful: the Negritos, a stone age people hidden in distant jungle hills; and mountain villagers who have had varying degrees of contact with modern influence. The second group is thought to represent the second wave of early immigration to the Philippines, from Indonesia between a thousand and five thousand years ago. Later arrivals, Malays from Borneo and Malaya, settled in the lowlands and are now, in the main, the modern Filipinos.

The mountain people—such as Bontoc and Kalinga groups of Luzon's Mountain Province—resisted European influence for centuries. More recently they have had varying contact with Catholic and Protestant missionaries from Europe and the United States, and with the central government. Many have been to school, and some have graduated from universities. A few have reached high positions in the civil service, the armed forces, or the churches. Yet there are still people in the less accessible villages following a way of life which owes very little to European or modern Filipino influence. Some of the more nationalistic young scholars are trying to encourage interest in, and respect for, these peoples and their cultures and artifacts.

Even the lowlanders of the sixteenth century lived in fragmented local societies. By comparison with the Aztec civilization, which the Spanish were busy destroying at roughly the same time, Philippine society was unspectacular. But it was not negligible. The magnificent rice terraces of Banaue in the Mountain Province are one of the wonders of Asia. They were built perhaps as long as two thousand years ago.

103. Part of the extraordinary complex of rice terraces at Banaue in t Mountain Province (below). **104.** A young Kalinga woman at work (opposite).

The Kalingas and their neighbours were headhunters. Heads were still being taken regularly well within living memory. One or two still fall in local disputes. There was quite a vogue in Japanese heads during World War II. Under the influence of missionaries and the central government, head-taking is no longer the accepted way to win status, but village life is still recognizably pre-European. When a pig is brought as a gift to the villagers it is slaughtered ceremonially. Its liver and bile are examined for omens, by the elders. The men do the cooking on such occasions. Children eat first—delicacies of cooked offal. The women wait.

In the Mountain Province town of Bontoc, the Bontoc people occasionally put on a show for visitors in a copy of a traditional village built in the grounds of a mission school. They wear cloth in the vibrant colours and skilful weave for which the Bontoc are famous. They perform a propitiation dance to the ancient spirits. The men sit in a little compound behind a stone wall, an area traditionally reserved for the village elders. In the old days the heads of their enemies, enormously potent in magic, would be buried under the flagstones. It will need some sort of magic to preserve the culture of the mountain peoples much longer against the pressures of education, missionary work, and tourism. While they last they remind the modern Filipinos of how much they have gained from European contact, and how much they have lost in cultural self-confidence.

108. A woman of the
Bontoc people in Luzon's
Mountain Province (right).

A young Muslim
man in ceremonial dress
Basilan island, near the
southern island of
Mindanao.
Soldiers on hand in
Zamboanga city to keep the
peace.
Children in a Muslim
fishing village, Mindanao.
High on stilts is a
village of Muslim water
people near Zamboanga
(above).

One group of Filipinos with whom the Spanish never came to terms, peaceful or otherwise, were the Muslims of the south. By the time the Spanish arrived in the Philippines the Islamic religion had spread from Malaya and Indonesia through Borneo and as far north as the island of Mindanao. The Muslims of the southern sultanates were a warlike, piratical people much feared by other Filipinos. Muslim society was more tightly organized than were those in the other islands. The local sultans might squabble among themselves, but they united against the Spanish invaders. Through their religion they had access to other, sophisticated cultures. The Spanish could never come to terms with the Muslims as the Dutch and British did elsewhere, because of their insistence on trying to convert them to Christianity. It all seemed to the Spanish to be an echo of their long struggle in Europe and North Africa against the Moors. In fact they called the Muslims of the southern Philippines "Moros".

There was some penetration by missionaries, who even managed to convert a sultan, but generally they did not get very far. Spain built a fort in the city of Zamboanga on Mindanao, and exercised a tenuous control over the surrounding area. Zamboanga itself flourished as a trading centre, and a Christian community developed. The Spanish and later governments imported Christians from the northern islands to open up new land in Mindanao, which did nothing to appease the Muslims who thought they owned the land even if they had no new-fangled legal title to it.

The Americans, when their turn came to inherit the problem, even signed a separate treaty with the Muslims. But they had to keep troops on hand in Mindanao. So does the present government, whose policy has varied between military action and negotiation. Zamboanga itself seems secure, but visitors are not encouraged to wander much further afield. Some military actions in the Muslim islands have been savage, including the destruction of the city of Jolo, for centuries the centre of a powerful sultanate. On the other hand, amnesty terms offered to Muslim rebels by the central government are so generous that they have caused some jealousy among Christians in Mindanao. A problem which has been festering for four hundred years still defies easy solution.

It is possible in theory that the Philippines could have been a Chinese instead of a Spanish colony. There was a Chinese community long before the Spanish came; China was a great power, and had it wanted to could very likely have taken over the country fairly easily. But the emperors showed no interest in founding distant colonies.

The history of the Chinese community in the Philippines is so appalling that it is a wonder they are there at all. The Chinese were encouraged to settle, at the start of Spanish occupation, because the Filipinos had not enough skilled artisans or craftsmen and the Spanish would not demean themselves with physical labour. The Spanish regime, however, was obsessed with suspicions about the Chinese and about the intentions of China herself. They piled more and more restrictions on the Chinese until eventually they provoked resistance and protest. Spanish reaction was hysterical. Three times in the seventeenth and eighteenth centuries they massacred thousands of Chinese settlers and expelled the survivors. Three times they had to bring them back again because the economy would have collapsed without them. The Chinese provided for some two hundred years a large part of the skilled workforce and most of the entrepreneurs and money-managers.

There is still discrimination against them in matters of citizenship. They exercise a great deal of economic power, but politically they adopt a low profile. Like the Filipinos, however, the Chinese cannot avoid a certain flamboyance of style. One of the strangest examples of this is a quiet but apparently well-to-do township on the outskirts of Manila which is actually a Chinese cemetery. The houses are tombs. Families drive out at weekends and festivals to have a picnic lunch with their ancestors. The Chinese have certainly earned some sort of memorial to their part in creating the Philippine nation, and they might as well build it themselves.

One of the most important Chinese contributions was hidden for a while. The Chinese and the Spanish unwittingly cooperated in producing a highly significant group of people—the *mestizos*, that is people of Filipino blood mixed with Chinese, or Spanish, or both. By the nineteenth century there was a sizeable group of *mestizo* families

113. Houses which are actually tombs in the Chinese cemetery, Manila.

which formed the educated elite. They had money and leisure; in other words they had both the means and the time to think. They thought as Filipinos, and they began to wonder whether the benefits of Spanish rule were worth the cost.

Like all colonialists sooner or later, the Spanish prepared the way for their own demise. They needed an educated professional class of local people, and so created one—thereby producing also the potential leadership of revolt. In their administration they pursued policies which eventually provided the spark of revolt.

For two hundred and fifty years the mainstay of the Philippines was the galleon trade with Mexico. The Chinese brought silks and other rich textiles to the colony to be shipped on to Spain. Galleons from Mexico brought silver to pay for these goods. The trade ended after the successful Mexican revolt in 1810. While this trade went on, and after it, the Spanish gradually built up an agricultural cash economy in the Philippines. Tobacco and sugar plantations, timber concessions and ricefields flourished, but in the main, except for a few elite families, the Filipinos had no stake in them. They provided labour under a system similar to feudal tenure. Landowners were frequently oppressive—and they included the religious orders, which had large grants of land.

Even in religious matters the Filipinos were held down. Spain was reluctant to train a native clergy, both through racial prejudice, and because of some unfortunate experiences in Mexico. Graft and corruption were rife in some parts of the church and in officialdom.

Besides all this, events in Europe began to bear down on the distant colony. Between 1800 and 1875 there was chronic revolution in Spain; the country swung between monarchy and republic, conservative and liberal regimes. Every time the government changed so did the top level of officials in the Philippines. The colony had forty governors in seventy-five years. Errors, prejudices, and confusion all led to the first revolution in modern Asia.

The revolution proper started in 1896 although there had been sporadic outbreaks before that, vigorously put down. Various secret societies were active among the Filipinos. Some had links with European freemasonry, and many were anti-clerical. Their leaders were mainly intellectuals, but many of these, especially the well-to-do ones, were after reforms rather than revolution.

The peasants rose in arms under the leadership of Emilio Aguinaldo, a school teacher turned general. Neither side could quite finish off the other. The Americans meanwhile were supporting Cuba in its war of independence against Spain, and had a fleet in Hong Kong watching events in the Philippines. When the United States declared war on Spain in 1898 the American fleet moved in, supposedly to help the Filipinos. General Aguinaldo declared independence—prematurely, as it turned out.

Under the treaty which ended their war with Spain the Americans acquired the former Spanish colony for an indemnity of $20 million. In effect they bought the Philippines. First, however, they had to take it from the Filipinos who thought they had just won independence. The Filipino-American war was brief. Except for local skirmishing it was all over by 1900, and the Philippines began its second period of colonial rule, this time under the Americans.

There are some curious aspects to all this. Not the least of them is what the Americans thought they were doing, acquiring a distant colony by force of arms when they were supposed to be the world's foremost champions of freedom. They were taking what they wanted, which was a staging post for the China trade, a source of raw material, and a market. President McKinley's government had to make this acceptable to those Americans who actually believed in their national altruism. The silent majority was assured, therefore, that America was fulfilling her manifest destiny by taking up the white man's burden in the Philippines. The unspoken justification for this was social Darwinism, the view of evolutionary white supremacy which was fashionable, and useful, at the time.

The other curious thing is that in Filipino popular history to this day the emotional emphasis is heavily on the revolution against

Spain, not the war of resistance against America; and the revolution is notably and ironically celebrated in the person of a man who opposed it—Jose Rizal.

Rizal came of a rich Chinese *mestizo* family of sugar planters. He studied medicine in Manila and Spain, spoke several European languages, had some talent as an artist, and was in general a most cultivated man. In 1882 and 1891 he published two novels which exposed the miserable life of many Filipinos and blamed not only the Spanish, but the Filipinos themselves. He urged his fellow countrymen to self-improvement and told them to stop being so servile.

Rizal was suspected of revolutionary plotting, and was packed off to exile in Mindanao, where he worked as a doctor. He was in touch with a revolutionary group, but Rizal refused to join a plot for the violent overthrow of the Spanish. He believed the Filipinos were not ready to govern themselves properly.

When the Cubans began their revolt, Rizal offered to serve as a doctor on the Spanish side. He actually set sail for Cuba but was recalled before he got there. He was charged with incitement to rebellion and was found guilty by a military court. Rizal wrote, in prison, a very moving poem of farewell to his sweetheart and his country. He was shot in the back by a firing squad, as a traitor, on 30 December 1896. He died bravely, at the age of thirty-five.

It is not surprising that the Spanish have a rather shifty look in the paintings which march solemnly round the walls of the Rizal Museum, in the grounds of Fort Santiago's ruins. The whole Rizal episode was more the result of colonialist paranoia than of any rabid intent on the part of Rizal himself. He seems to have been a gradualist, or a meliorist, or whatever word later revolutionaries might have used to describe a well-meaning bourgeois. Yet a Rizal cult flourished in the Philippines, and still does. The romantic side of Rizal's character, expressed in his poetry and novels as well as in his life, is no doubt partly responsible for that; there may be other reasons also.

Renato Constantino, sociologist:

Rizal was one of the greatest men produced by our race. He was a martyr to Spanish bigotry. But our historic goal then, as now, was to free our people from colonial oppression, and in this regard Rizal failed miserably because he repudiated the Filipino revolution. The cult of Rizal was encouraged by the Americans in order to downgrade Filipino resistance leaders, genuine people's heroes, and to elevate Rizal to the status of a national hero. As a result of American educational policies the Filipinos have suffered from a crisis of identity. After some indulgence in self-examination many Filipinos are uneasy about their identity. That is why there is now a tendency on the part of some sectors to revive interest in our cultural minority. This is a regressive step and a romantic adventure which diverts attention from the real source of our identity, which is the struggle against colonialism.

The city of Baguio, a summer mountain resort north of Manila, is a pleasant reflection of the middle American style, with its broad sidewalks, parks, and imitation West Point. The new influence was much more relaxed, practical, and worldly than that of the Spanish, and it was more widely spread.

114. Cadets of the Philippine Military Academy, Baguio—an imitation West Point.

The Americans early declared their intention of leading the Philippines to independence. George Washington joined Dr. Rizal in the heroes' pantheon. Secular state schools were opened all over the islands. English was taught widely and enthusiastically, and became the language of higher learning, thus enriching the education of those who learned the language easily and restricting the opportunities of those who did not.

Church and state were separated. Religious freedom was guaranteed, and Protestant missionaries arrived. The Filipino interest in religion and religiosity blossomed into an exotic variety of sects. Nowadays there are more than two hundred and fifty.

Political parties appeared early in the American period. A senate and a house of representatives were formed in 1916 with elected majorities, a small franchise, and limited powers. Land was reserved for Filipino cultivators. Filipinos were trained in modern business methods, and Filipino landlords were transformed into capitalists.

The corporation replaced the hacienda. Tenants in many areas became employees—not feudal vassals any longer, but still a landless peasantry and a seedbed for later discontents. American capital and American commercial interests were given highly privileged positions.

Understandably the Americans believed that their own social system was the ideal model. The Filipinos were not reluctant, and the life style for the new money acquired a strong American flavour while the older elite showed, and still shows, more Spanish influence. Filipino intellectuals had access to the best in American culture, while the mass media copied its more popular style, and still do.

The Philippines became a Commonwealth in 1935, with its own president and a promise from the United States of independence within ten years. But that progress was interrupted by war.

The Philippines suffered more damage during World War II than any other Asian country except Burma. It was fought over savagely twice. During Japanese occupation Filipino guerilla bands roamed the islands, exacting a considerable toll with ambush and sabotage. The guerillas fought bravely, and produced some notable war heroes. The most decorated was Ferdinand E. Marcos.

Ferdinand E. Marcos, president of the Philippines:

I have always felt that the Second World War was a preparation for the new leadership that was to take over the republic of the Philippines. It was a warning—the war saw the commonwealth of the Philippines tested and tried. The old leadership was actually eliminated by the war. We lost a million men, and this generation that was trained into the conflict, that was later to be known as the underground movement in the Philippines against the Japanese, spawned the new leadership of the Philippines. They are now actually the leaders on the national and local levels. The same thing still with the people—while there were some vices that came out of the war, the war did bring out the resilience of the people, their patriotism, their love of country.

115. President Marcos.

On their side the Japanese talked about cooperation for prosperity, while ripping out of the Philippines every piece of raw material they could lift. There were some Filipino collaborators, and the Japanese set up a puppet regime. The dungeons of Fort Santiago got a new lease of death, being used for the imprisonment, torture, and murder of hundreds of Filipinos and others. Some terrible things were done, and the Filipinos have carefully recorded them on notice boards scattered about the ruins of the old fort. This lends a certain piquancy to the happy snaps of today's crowds of Japanese tourists. The Filipinos don't mind—or if they do, they are careful not to show it. They need tourists and capital, and modern Japan is a major source of both.

There are other reminders of unhappy times, such as the monument to twenty-five thousand men who died on the death march from Bataan to prison camps.

The end of the war brought the Americans back—this time as friends and liberators. Despite the hesitations of some American business interests the Philippines became an independent republic on 4 July 1946.

After the war the guerillas who had fought the Japanese emerged as heroes. Among them were the communist-led Hukbalahap, or Huks. In 1946 some of the Huks stood for the new congress, and six were elected. But they were prevented from taking their seats and were later expelled from the congress. The excuse was a charge of fraud at the polls; the reason was more complicated.

The new Philippine government was bankrupt and desperately needed financial aid. It was known that the Huks' six votes would have prevented passage of a bill to accept such aid from the United States in return for various advantages for American trade and industry. So the Huks were kept out. This cynical action intensified the guerilla problem, which was one reason given for the imposition of martial law in the Philippines nearly thirty years later. Moreover, the Philippines has been ever since among those nations which have never found a place for the left in the mainstream of political life.

The terms of independence maintained tariff and investment advantages for the United States. The peso was linked to the U.S. dollar, making the Philippines a safe market for American goods. A separate agreement required the Philippines to provide facilities for American naval and military bases. In return the Philippines received $1,240 million rehabilitation aid, ships, arms and ammunition, and an assumption of a special relationship with the United States. The Filipinos were helped enormously by American aid. In return they were expected to provide a shop window in Asia for the American system.

The special relationship cushioned the Filipinos' emergence as an independent people into the world of the cold war. But it also meant that they were still a client of the United States, politically and economically. It meant, too, that their credentials as Asians were suspect. They were a Malay people who were in danger of being regarded as imitation Americans with Spanish names. That stung, and still does.

President Marcos:

As far as I am concerned I have no question about my identity. I know where I come from. I know the purpose for which I was created by God. I belong to the Filipino race. I belong to a race which has always sought freedom. I belong to a race which believes itself equal to any other race in the world. I don't say this in arrogance, but I believe I speak for all Filipinos when I say this, and for this reason, perhaps, we can claim that we are the only Southeast Asian country that actually fought the Japanese in the last world war.

In the 1950s the Filipinos borrowed the idea of manifest destiny, and decided that theirs was to provide a bridge between Asia and the West. The idea foundered, not only because it was romantic, but also because serious weaknesses began to emerge in Filipino society.

Some of these weaknesses were the dark side of otherwise admirable things, such as the warmth and strength of Filipino family life. Family relationships are very close and extensive, as they have been since long before the Spanish came. The family relationship is important so early in life, and maintained and cherished so carefully, that a need for it is extended into the world outside the family. Filipinos look for relationships involving a kind of familial dependence and indulgent authority, which makes for pleasant relationships. It also, despite the warmth and innocence of its beginnings, opens the way to nepotism, patronage, and personal factions in political life.

The charm of the Filipinos, both individually and as a people enjoying a distinctive way of life, is inescapable. There is a great deal to be said for an expansive sense of fun and display. But that too has its other side.

Professor Emmanuel Torres, art gallery director, Ateneo University, Quezon City:

To my mind the flamboyant spirit of the Filipinos is a sign of their largely anti-rational tendencies. It is certainly characteristic of the strong emotional impulse, this undercurrent of desire to put trust in something intuitive, and part of this is directed also towards any kind of charismatic leadership or charismatic object—in other words an object that is symbolic of supernatural powers. This kind of desire to be attracted to a charismatic figure is probably what underlies the psychology of a lot of Filipinos of the working class and peasantry who want to believe in psy-

116. Flamboyance and ingenuity—a Volkswagen body made of wrought iron and wire, Manila (above).

chic phenomena, psychic experiences like psychic surgery. Then of course one can look at this flamboyant side of the Filipinos from another angle; to my mind it is expressive of Filipino optimism which I think makes them a very flexible people.

The phenomenon of psychic surgery encapsulates the ordinary Filipino's faith, superstition, and taste for involvement in melodrama. The healers supposedly enter the body without the use of instruments but through the magical power contained in their fingers. Most of them have associations with religious sects, and ascribe this power to the Holy Spirit. The operations are conjuring tricks involving the extremely skilful use of animal blood and tissue, and sometimes of quite bizarre foreign bodies supposedly removed from the patient's vitals— but they do sometimes work. Symptoms disappear when, presumably, the expectation is strong enough or the performance persuasive enough. But it may not work for long.

117. Against the faraway background of modern Manila is the Tondo, an infamous slum area.
118. A Manila "psychic surgeon" operating on a patient.
119. Narrow alley in a Manila slum.

By the beginning of the 1970s it was becoming clear that illusions do not work for long in government, either. The symptoms of sickness did not go away. Powerful landed interests, a legacy of the Spanish era, were enmeshed with a corrupt political life. Some politicians had private armies, and affected a style which would not have been out of place in the Chicago of the 1920s. In many parts of the country the rural economic system was little better than feudal. The Communist

120. One of the innumerable small boys who hawk cigarettes to motorists beside Manila's main roads.

Party, though illegal, had a military arm and was urging revolution. There were suspicions that right-wing interests might strike first with a coup d'état. Either way the Philippines faced civil war. That, at any rate, was the scenario as described later by President Marcos. So—martial law.

Only a Filipino president, perhaps, could describe the imposition of martial law as "a democratic revolution from the centre". It shows a certain flair. The aim is said to be a "New Society". We shall have to wait to see what that turns out to mean. One thing it will have to mean is a firmer sense of what it is to be a Filipino. The ambivalence of an educated elite between Eastern race and Western culture is being attacked at the moment through Western analysis. It might be better to try some Eastern resignation.

An identity crisis, like teenage acne, is a sign of certain natural processes going on. It sorts itself out, but while it lasts it is a real problem.

The first step to maturity could be to recognize an identifiable national Filipino character, and accept it. The signs of it are all around. It should be attractive enough for anyone, once the spots have gone.

6 Thailand

Do Good, Receive Good; Do Evil, Receive Evil
(Thai proverb)

The Thais are devout followers of a compassionate Buddha, but theirs is in some ways a violent society with a violent history. Thais respect the Buddhist teaching that the ways to enlightenment involve abandoning worldly desires, yet their capital city is notorious as a flesh-peddlar's paradise. The country is a democracy in theory, with a long history of corrupt and authoritarian rule in practice.

The character of Thai society is a puzzle. The keys to understanding it are Buddhism and the monarchy. It is easy to misunderstand it, as some Americans did when they said the Thais were the nicest people money could buy. But that was in the days when they were doing the buying, or thought they were.

Nobody buys the Thais. They are their own men, and proud of it. Thai society, with all its odd contrasts, is one they have made themselves. Alone in their region of Asia they have never known colonial rule. The word Thai means "free".

Thailand is almost entirely Buddhist—more than 90 per cent. About half the adult male population has spent at least some time in a monastery. To become an ordained monk for about three months at the age of twenty or so is a popular way of gaining maturity, a rite of passage into adulthood.

The permanent monks are an enormously influential group, not because they guide and interfere in worldly affairs, but precisely because they do not. In Japan, by way of contrast, the many Buddhist sects run a sort of spiritual supermarket with competing products shrewdly marketed. But not in Thailand. There are only two sects and the difference is inscrutable to the layman. The monk's concentration is on earning rebirth in a higher station, or on the hope of enlightenment—not the lay public's, but his own.

The Buddhism in Thailand is of the Theravada or southern school. Its nature has much to do with the kind of people the Thais are, even with the unstable political scene in Bangkok. Both Buddhism and the Thai people themselves came to Thailand from elsewhere. The Thais originated in southern China, around Yunnan. Their race and language are akin to the Chinese. Under pressure from northern peoples they moved south in stages beginning about the sixth century B.C. They were a recognizable nation by the thirteenth century.

121. Buddha figures line the wall of a cloister in a Bangkok monastery.

Buddhism travelled eastwards from India in two streams. The Mahayana or northern school followed the Silk Road to China, Korea, and Japan. The more austere Theravada school came from Ceylon and southern India.

At the centre of the Thai religion is the idea of making merit. It is earned by performing worthy or devout deeds, especially by helping the Order of Monks. Merit accrues like a savings account without interest, and counts towards a better fate in another incarnation.

A popular way to make merit is to give the monks their daily food, at dawn. Before first light long lines of monks are to be seen threading their way through streets near the temples, picking up food along established routes from devout householders. In the central plains they make the daily journey in small boats, calling at rice farmers' and fishermen's houses. Others, in city and country, wait patiently in line outside the temple gates for the food-givers to arrive and set up small stalls rather in the manner of an army field canteen. Every monk is treated with respect, simply by virtue of being a monk. A woman must not touch him directly; he carries a cloth to prevent her hands from touching his. The monks show no reaction to the gifts of food because they are supposed to be indifferent to material things. They offer no thanks, because it is the giver who benefits from the exchange by making merit.

Merit is also made by releasing birds caged for the purpose and sold to the merit-makers. To suggest that it might be better not to cage the birds in the first place is to miss the point, according to the Thais. The bird *is in* the cage, and to let it out is a kindly act. Some Thai fishermen have a similarly engaging argument. They do not kill fish, because their religion forbids killing. They just put the fish on the river bank, and if it dies it's a pity to waste it.

All Buddhists are meant to live at the very least by the Five Precepts: abstinence from destroying life, from stealing, from fornication, from speaking falsely, and from drinking strong liquor. They are obeyed, probably, to much the same extent as the Ten Commandments in Christian societies. In any case laymen following only these minimum rules have no hope of reaching Nirvana, the state of pure enlightenment, the void, release from the weary cycle of rebirth. The monks have such a chance, in theory.

They follow 227 ascetic rules to help remove them from the temptations of the lay world. They take vows of poverty and chastity. They have no possessions to speak of, only their robes, a foodbowl, a razor, and suchlike necessities.

Few monks have pretensions to serious scholarship. Entrance qualifications are low, and not many pick their way through examinations to the highest grades in the order. For some, the Order of

Monks is a ladder for moving up in society. It is not unusual for a bright but poor young man to take advantage of the schooling and of the contacts made possible by his prestige as a monk, and to emerge into a good secular job. Monks may enter and leave the order at any time.

A department of religious affairs keeps a register of monks' names and issues each one with an identity tag. Monks may not join anti-government political activity and no communist may become a monk. The monkhood is centralized, and in a sense nationalized. This puts a dead hand on philosophical speculation. The stress is on testable learning, not on the fruits of meditation. Although, of course, there is meditation, and some monks specialize in its techniques.

Thai Buddhism is not dogmatic, it is passive and tolerant. It tolerates relics of earlier religions. A spirit dance performed regularly by lay people in the grounds of a Buddhist temple in Chieng Mai, northern Thailand, is an example of this tolerance. The villagers dance in with flowers, behind drums and flutes, to worship the spirit of the monastery grounds under a *bodhi* tree. They also worship the tree itself as the home of a tree spirit and as a Buddhist symbol, since it was under a *bodhi* tree that the Lord Buddha received enlightenment. Last, the dancers worship at the *jedi*, the container of sacred Buddhist relics.

Some temples have spirit houses on the border of their grounds to propitiate the spirit of the land on which the monks have built. The lay people put them up; the monks look the other way.

Almost every house, hotel, and business block has its spirit house.

124. Spirit houses erected by villagers on the margin of temple land on the central plains near Suphanburi.

Some of them, especially those in front of modern tourist hotels, are large and splendidly decorated. The more modest domestic spirit houses have a social use as a safety valve. Members of the household, especially the women, will soothe their nerves after a domestic upset by telling their troubles to the spirit and asking forgiveness for flying off the handle. It is cheaper than tranquilizers and probably, if you believe in it, just as effective.

Modern, sophisticated Thais, and Buddhists at that, are not supposed to believe in spirits lurking in trees and under the ground their house is built on. But they do—in a way. They are hedging their bets, like the Christians who fear bad luck if they break a mirror or walk under a ladder.

Another example of the elasticity of Thai attitudes is the status of women. The Buddhist view, or at least its implication, is that women are inferior because they epitomize those sensual pleasures which are likely to trip a man up on his way to spiritual advancement. The respectful forms of address which many Thai women use to their husbands also suggest some inherent superiority of the male. And yet Thai women in fact have a considerable degree of equality both in law and in terms of ordinary behaviour. They can inherit family property equally with men, and have similar freedom to seek divorce.

125. A young Thai woman.

In Bangkok middle-class circles there are many highly successful women competing on an equal footing with men, without social disapproval. In hospitals, for instance, patients submit confidently to the ministrations of many women doctors. A large advertising agency has a woman in charge of making television commercials. More surprisingly, Thailand is ahead of many Western countries in having that talisman of conservatism and propriety, a bank, run entirely by women. A large branch of the Bangkok Bank has ninety-two bank officers and other staff. They are all women, from the security guards to the manager. Most of the bank's customers are men.

Thai society is flexible. It rolls, smiling, with the punches, as it did during World War II. Thailand, having little choice, gave Japanese troops the right of passage in 1941, and obligingly declared war on Britain and the United States. Three years later, when it was clear that the Japanese were going to lose, Bangkok was thick with British and American agents operating with the full knowledge of the Thai government.

It is not hard to make that kind of flexibility sound like hypocrisy. Sometimes it is, but not usually. It is an important part of Thai social attitudes, and it has a lot to do with a peculiar Thai word—*sanuk*. There is no exact translation. It means something like "relaxation", "warmth", "having a good time". It has a wide application. "What did you do last night?" "*Sanuk.*"—Had a good time. "What's your new job like?" "*Sanuk.*"—Pleasant relationships.

The word, the attitude, are partly defensive. The Thais like all Asian peoples will avoid blunt confrontation whenever they can. Confrontations involve face, and loss of face can lead to violence. People smile often, but they do not always mean only to be friendly. The air of *sanuk*, the elaborate courtesies, the smiling acquiescence, are all very pleasant. They are also a way of avoiding conflict, of evading the vanity-wounding clash of wills which might call up the impulse to violence.

There are good practical reasons for calmness and harmony. Village life depends on cooperation, especially in the complicated systems of wet-rice irrigation, and open feuding would make it impossible. Buddhist teachings reinforce the need for serenity. Anger and hatred are sinful and weigh in the debit side of the merit scales. But the Thais, like the rest of us, need some release from the repression of aggressive feelings. This no doubt explains the peculiar savagery of Thai boxing, in which the contestants use feet and knees as well as fists to pummel each other and raise the roars of the crowd.

Despite doctrine and diversion there is a fast-growing rate of violent crime in Thailand. Murders are said to be cheap and easy to arrange, especially in Bangkok.

126. Thai boxers can use
their feet and do, with
bruising effect.

Bangkok is where generalizations about Thai society begin to wear
thin. The capital looks like much the same sort of rat-race as any
other huge, overcrowded city, and in many ways it is. Western
materialist values are more powerful there than in the countryside.
The middle class learns to be competitive and urban life breaks down
conservative rural verities. But the people of Bangkok are still Thais.
There may be a certain tension behind the smiles, but there is still a
pleasant amount of *sanuk*.

127. The gilded jedi spire
symbolizes the quest for
enlightenment, made no
easier by the busy pace of
modern commercial
Bangkok.

The Thais as a people have an air of relaxation, of detachment, in the face of life's difficulties which is the envy of some more frantic societies. However, this very detachment is the despair of sterner spirits among the Thais themselves. One such spirit is the Lord Abbott of Djitta Bhawan, a monastery and spiritual battle school near Bangkok, who preaches a kind of muscular Buddhism extolling the virtues of hard work and self-reliance. The Lord Abbott has a strong personality, which in a more worldly context might be authoritarian, and some right-wing political connections.

Revival movements and ginger groups pop up in Thai Buddhism from time to time, as in other faiths. This one seems unusually energetic, and obviously has some rich supporters. It has splendid buildings, designed by the Lord Abbott himself, as its headquarters. Djitta Bhawan draws clergy and lay people from all over Thailand, often in their hundreds, for inspirational courses. Apart from their theological content, a main concern of the courses seems to be that Buddhism has grown flabby and that monks must build and work with their own hands.

128. Young monks labouring outside the revivalist monastery of Djitta Bhawan.

A different attempt to stir up the Buddhist church is being made by a group of lay intellectuals in Bangkok. This campaign has no grand headquarters of its own, but it does have the support of the Buddhist hierarchy. Academics, writers, and other laymen lecture to monks from various parts of the country about the problems of social change.

Sulak Sivakasa, publisher:

The reason for this monk-training project is that the monks have in the past been a very useful part of the society. The temple has been the centre of all activities, cultural, intellectual, not to mention spiritual. But the monks seem to be losing their leadership qualities once the society becomes more and more urbanized. So we have to warn them that urbanization is a fact, that they cannot deny it. Urbanization is going to reach them wherever they are, so we try to make them aware of the social problems in the big towns, of the urbanization process. Once they see all that, they have got to decide for themselves. In a way we try to "conscientize" them so they themselves must decide what their role may be in order to retain their leadership qualities. If they can do that the future of the Buddhist Church, the future of the country, will be much more pleasant. But if they fail in this I don't know what to think for the future.

It is common for groups of families in villages or suburbs to join together in holding a merit-making ceremony. A small party of monks will obligingly turn up to chant prayers and receive gifts. Presenting the monks with new robes or foodbowls at such ceremonies is regarded as being more meritorious than the routine daily foodgiving. Cooperation for basically selfish purposes is one thing, but close involvement with other people's lives and problems is quite another. The thrust of Theravada Buddhism is against such involvement.

Everyone is responsible for his own salvation. The way lies through separation from material possessions, worldly ambitions, and normal human desires. Every opinion is open to doubt. No one has a right to impose his own views on others. The world we live in is not the "real" world, and all ideologies about how to organize it are delusions.

This atmosphere clouds the Thai intellectual climate. It saps the confidence of political parties and trade unions. It makes it difficult to develop the kind of social organizations which modern Western societies have found necessary. The Thais are a nation of non-joiners. So what is it that holds together this collection of individualists— what makes the Thai people into a nation at all?

The cement of Thai society is the monarchy. The history of the kings of Thailand, or Siam as it used to be, has run for seven hundred years through various dynasties, with elaborate style and formality.

The present monarch, King Phumiphon, has a more popular touch. So have the crown prince, who was trained in Australia as an army officer, and the two princesses. But the king's aura as the focus of nationhood is no less.

The Thais manage to reconcile individualism and detachment with acceptance of a hierarchical social system. They understand social relationships in terms of higher and lower status, with sets of formal manners and styles of speech to suit all occasions. At the apex of all the hierarchies is the king. He is semi-divine, protected by magic and sacred ritual according to ideas the Brahmans brought from India many centuries ago. The king is at the very centre of what it means to be a Thai. The Thai word for history actually means "biography of the kings".

The monarchy has been constitutional since a bloodless coup in 1932, when it dawned on some of the intelligentsia, especially a few educated in republican France, that absolute monarchies were out of date. With one three-year interruption which ended in 1976, however, government since the coup has been by imposed, authoritarian regimes, a mixture of military rule and rule by an entrenched bureaucracy which has grown steadily in power as various military leaders have come and gone.

The reasons why the Thai people put up with this for so long involve a set of unifying ideas which have to do with the king, and with Buddhism. The king is venerated by practically every group. All the comings and goings of field marshals and prime ministers have left the monarchy intact, giving a sense of unity and continuity above politics.

Buddhism has encouraged people to think in this way—in "compartments". People of higher social status have earned it by making merit in a previous existence. They have a right to it. Government, therefore, is a matter for those who govern. Everyone's main concern is for his own fate, and the way things fall out otherwise is a just and natural order. Governments may not always be precisely obeyed, because individualism is strong, but on the whole they will be respected, because this shared social attitude is even stronger.

It is the forms, the institutions of government that are respected, rather than individual people in office. The exception to that is the king.

There have been more than twenty coups d'état in Thailand since 1932, all of them involving different cliques within the ruling elite. Thailand has no history of popular revolt. The various regimes have inherited the king's absolute power, but not his prestige.

The royal prestige is put to some specific uses, such as the encouragement of modernization in agriculture. The king uses a large part of the enormous grounds of his Bangkok palace as a research farm. The most colourful example of royal action with a direct purpose is the visit which the king makes each year, with Queen Sirikit, to the hill tribes of northern Thailand.

The king's person is sacred, and the ceremonies of welcome in a northern hill village are similar to those the animist villagers would use to honour the spirit of a great tree. Northern Thailand is part of what is known as the Golden Triangle, the source of at least half the world's illicit opium trade. Opium from the border of southern China and the northern tips of Burma, Thailand, and Laos, seeps down on to world markets through Thailand, with the connivance of corrupt officials. There are too many powerful fingers in the pot for the traffic to be stopped easily.

The king is encouraging the northern tribes to stop growing the opium poppy and to turn to other cash crops. The difficulty, of course, is in finding crops which pay as well. His other purpose is to draw the northern tribes more closely into the Thai family, as a counter to the enticements of communist missionaries from Laos.

129, 130. King Phumiphon and Queen Sirikit during the royal couple's annual visit to the northern hill tribes.

The early history of the Thai people was one of southward movement. The northern provincial capital of Chieng Mai was the capital of an independent Thai state in the thirteenth century. A flood of Thai people had moved south to escape the boisterous attentions of Kublai Khan in southern China. The site for Chieng Mai is said to have been chosen by Providence. Two white deer and five white mice were seen together in a jungle clearing—an omen too powerful to ignore. King Mengrai, the leader of the infant state, raided Burma, bringing back workers in gold, silver, and bronze, and other craftsmen. The craft work of Chieng Mai is still famous.

The Burmese captured Chieng Mai in 1556, leaving their mark. Inside a local temple a decrepit pavilion houses a large Burmese Buddha which the proud Thais have allowed to slide into decay. Among the elaborate ornamentation of the same temple a Burmese lion holds a Thai in his mouth, showing who was boss. The Burmese held Chieng Mai for two hundred years. Chieng Mai was not the only independent Thai state. Another, also founded in the thirteenth century, had its capital some way south at Sukhothai. It flourished briefly, then moved south again to Ayuthaya.

131. A Burmese lion holds a Thai in its mouth—part of the decoration of an old temple in Chieng Mai, the northern Thai capital once occupied by the Burmese.
132. The large Burmese Buddha in the temple of Chieng Mai (right).

Ayuthaya was the Thai capital for four hundred years, a city of great splendour. The Thais were involved in almost incessant warfare with their old enemies the Burmese, with their other neighbours the Khmers, and occasionally among themselves. Khmer captives influenced by Indian culture formed a kind of intellectual booty, educating their captors as the Greeks did the Romans. Thirty-three kings reigned in Ayuthaya. Scholarship and Buddhist arts flourished, and so did the military arts.

Thailand has a long history of warfare, but no popular tradition of militarism. To the people warfare was something to be performed reluctantly when their rulers told them to. It was really a matter for kings. Even the kings took the point. In 1592 King Naresuan of Ayuthaya defeated the crown prince of Burma in single combat, mounted on elephants.

In 1767 Ayuthaya fell to the Burmese, and was destroyed and looted. The king and therefore the capital moved south again to Thonburi and then across the river to Bangkok, "City of Angels". The Burmese were eventually driven off and the modern Thai dynasties began. Ayuthaya was crucial to the history of the Thais, and not only

133, 134 The ruins of a temple in Ayuthaya, scene of former glories.

for its battles and now-faded glories. Ayuthaya was the scene of the first formal, continuing relationships between the Thais and the great powers of the Western world. First were the Portuguese with traders and missionaries, then the Dutch, the English, and the French. In 1624 a letter from Louis XIV of France was carried upriver to Ayuthaya in a gilded royal barge propelled by sixty oarsmen dressed in scarlet. The court gave land and other assistance for the building of Christian churches, but the Thais showed no more than a polite interest in what went on inside them.

The Ayuthaya period established an important image of the Kingdom of Siam in the eyes of the West. It was exotic, and splendid, and self-confident. This was not a collection of squabbling principalities ripe for a takeover and an enforced colonial unity. The Thais were already united. They were a nation, and they saw themselves as one.

Although two thirds of Thailand is forest, the basis of the nation has always been the rice-farming village. More than 80 per cent of the forty million Thais live in farming communities. The rice farmers of the central plains have a long history of independent landholding. Thailand has no big group of landless peasants. Unlike the Chinese, the Thais have a loosely structured society without emphasis on ancestors or extensive ties of kinship. They have had surnames for only fifty years or so, imposed by royal decree.

135. A small village temple overlooks a busy rice harvest in Thailand's central plains (below).

136—39. Life on the central plains of Thailand, near Suphanburi: a young farmer (opposite); using the breeze to winnow rice (above); fish traps along one of the vital waterways (centre); and a farmhouse kitchen (below).

140. Floating markets cater for housewives in village waterways all over the rice-growing lowlands and in Bangkok.

141. A "long-tail boat"—one of the thousands buzzing along Thailand's waterways. The whole engine and long propeller shaft turn for steering, as with an outboard motor.

The most respected people at village level are of course the monks of the local temple. The schoolteacher has some standing, as an educated man and a government officer. All old people are treated with respect. The elected headman of the village has formal respect too, but whether he has actual authority as well depends on personality as much as position. He is on the lowest rung of the government's administrative ladder, doing the job part-time for a small stipend. He is usually a fairly well-to-do farmer.

Rural Thai society is virtually classless. Some peasant farmers manage to acquire more land and money than their neighbours, but nobody translates this into terms of class or status. The poorest man in the village, if he served for many years as a monk, will far outrank in prestige a rich farmer with no temple service at all.

The view from the ricefields is on the whole a pleasant one. Even a little self-satisfied. "There's fish in the water," the Thais say, "there's rice in the fields." It is true. The good life, in a modest version, is available to most rural Thais. A man can work his own land, support his own family, mind his own business, and seek his own salvation. It seems to be a life lived largely without envy. Whether this can survive the influence of Western values is another matter.

The Thais have always tried to take only what they needed from the West. But no society has been able to keep that up. Attitudes and values spin off from the imports, whether of military bases, industrial capital, languages, or tourists. Thai society is old enough and strong enough to bend foreign notions into odd shapes—especially political ideas, and especially in Bangkok. Ideas of social equality are meaningless to a man who knows perfectly well that he is not the equal of anyone who is much older than he is, or who served as a monk for longer than he did, or who holds an official position. Democracy is a difficult idea to graft on to an ingrained deference to elders and betters. So the imported ideas are bent to fit.

What Westerners confidently identify as corruption, being quite familiar with it, a Thai might regard as no more than a natural perquisite for a man in high office. Elections are held according to democratic theory, and votes are bought and sold, newspaper editors terrorized, and candidates occasionally murdered, according to local practice.

Some groups do push for local practice to come closer to the ideals behind the ideas. In 1973 Bangkok students led demonstrations which persuaded the military regime to step down, or at least to step back, so that civilian politicians could take the front of the stage. But the generals were still there in the wings, and emerged again in October 1976 to impose martial law. The occasion was a savage battle between rightist and leftist students at one of Bangkok's university campuses. The trigger was the return of the exiled former strongman, Field Marshal Thanom Kittikachorn, who entered a monastery to make merit for his sick and ageing father. The background intrigue was obscure. It was clear, however, that the student groups were surrogates for the real antagonists: on the right most of the army, the bureaucrats, and the conservative parties; on the left the liberal and socialist parties and the infant labour movement.

The students had been unable to maintain the unity they had in 1973. After their success then they split into factions popularly known as the Action Group and the Conservative Group. Both were infiltrated and manipulated by interests outside the campuses. It seems unlikely that student groups will be encouraged to flourish under the latest regime.

Many students, especially those headed for the civil service, will maintain some informal links. The ties between student and teacher, and between classmates, are very influential. Getting on or getting anything done in Bangkok depends heavily on patronage, influence, and financial persuasion.

There is one cohesive, organized social group which Thailand shares with every other Southeast Asian country: the Chinese. There is a long history of Chinese immigration to Thailand, and more assimilation into the local society than anywhere else in the region. An estimated 15 per cent of. the Thai people, including the king, have some Chinese blood.

The Chinese were encouraged for centuries to come to Thailand, since the Thais themselves were reluctant to take on anything but agricultural work. Restrictions were imposed on the Chinese this century. There are still restraints on landholding and some occupations, but various political attempts to whip up anti-Chinese feeling have had little success outside Bangkok, and even here relationships generally seem equable. The Chinese are very powerful economically, but not at all anxious to pop their heads up politically.

Everything revolves around Bangkok. Where the king is, there is the nation. Even more so when the government, the bureaucracy, and the most elevated of the Buddhist hierarchs are there as well. Centralism is inescapable for the Thais, and it has disadvantages. Bangkok takes the urban increase which might otherwise be spread among several large cities. Slums grow, the crime rate soars. Centralism increases the sense of injustice of some distant groups, such as the Muslim Malays of the south, whose claims to special treatment have to be forced on the capital.

This life may be an illusion, as the Buddha teaches, but the Thais see no reason why they should not enjoy it. Night time is very *sanuk*. Diversions of every kind are for sale, some of them illegal even in

142. Bars and nightclubs line both sides of Patpong, a street in Bangkok known to most tourists.

Bangkok. The more genteel end of the massage parlour business is legal, and highly popular not only with tourists but with the Thais themselves. And why not? Urban life, industrial growth, and an occasional experiment in democracy are producing strains and tensions the rice-paddies never knew.

The Lord Buddha was walking in the moonlight just before dawn, so a story goes, when he met a woman carrying some food to offer to a tree spirit. The woman mistook the Buddha for a tree spirit, and offered him the food. He could have told her she was mistaken and refused the food, but he didn't. He took it. Why? For complicated theological reasons? No. Simply because it was offered.

The Thais like that story. A tolerant, easygoing religion; a tolerant, easygoing people. And very nice, too, on the travel posters. But if that is the Thailand you want to see, you need to be quick.

The pressures for change are irresistible—not so much from outside, although there are some problems there, but from inside: simply the momentum of Thai society itself moving slowly towards modernity. They may not get there, but if they do it will be at some cost. The comings and goings of the generals can interrupt this movement, and slow it down. But whether they can stop it altogether is another matter.

The Thais are feeling their way in the familiar, Western direction of material advantages, a large, acquisitive middle class, powerful political parties and trade unions.

There's not much *sanuk* in that package.

Bibliography

Alatas, S.H. *Modernization and Social Change*. Sydney: Angus and Robertson, 1972.
Ali, S. Husin. *Malay Peasant Society and Leadership*. Kuala Lumpur: Oxford University Press, 1975.
Arcilla, J.S. *An Introduction to Philippine History*. Quezon City: Ateneo de Manila University Press, 1973.
Benedict, Ruth. *The Chrysanthemum and the Sword: Patterns of Japanese Culture*. New York: World Publishing, 1967.
Black, Star, ed. *Guide to Malaysia*. Hong Kong: Apa Production, 1974.
Blanchard, W. *Thailand*. New Haven: H.R.A.F. Press, 1958.
Bloodworth, D. *An Eye for the Dragon*. Harmondsworth, Penguin, 1975.
Bunce, W.K., ed. *Religions in Japan*. Tokyo: Tuttle, 1955.
Bunnag, Jane. *Buddhist Monk Buddhist Layman*. London: Cambridge University Press, 1973.
Clemens, J., ed. *Discovering Macau*. Hong Kong: Macmillan, 1972.
Cawed, Carmencita. *The Culture of the Bontoc Igorot*. Manila: M.C.S. Enterprises, 1972.
Condon, J.C. and Saito, Mitsuko, eds. *Intellectual Encounters with Japan*. Tokyo: Simul Press, 1974.
Constantino, R. *Identity and Consciousness: The Philippine Experience* (monograph). Quezon City: Malaya Books, 1974.
———. *Origin of a Myth* (monograph). Quezon City: Malaya Books, no date.
Costa, H. de la. *Asia and the Philippines*. Manila: Solidaridad, 1967.
———. *The Background of Nationalism and Other Essays*. Manila: Solidaridad, 1965.
Cushner, N.P. *The Isles of the West*. Quezon City: Ateneo de Manila University Press 1966.
Edwardes, M. *Asia in the European Age*. London: Thames and Hudson, 1961.
FitzGerald, C.P. *The Southern Expansion of the Chinese People*. Canberra: Australian National University Press, 1972.
Furnivall, J.S. *Experiment in Independence: The Philippines*. Manila: Solidaridad, 1974.
Gowing, P.G. *Islands Under the Cross*. Manila: National Council of Churches, 1967.
———. and Scott, W.H., eds. *Acculturation in the Philippines*. Quezon City: New Day, 1971.
Grant, B. *Indonesia*. Ringwood: Penguin, 1967.
Hearn, Lafcadio. *A Japanese Miscellany*. Tokyo: Tuttle, 1954.
Holt, Claire, ed. *Culture and Politics in Indonesia*. Ithaca: Cornell University Press, 1972.

Hughes, R. *Hong Kong: Borrowed Place—Borrowed Time*. New York: Praeger, 1968.

Hutton, P. *Guide to Java*. Hong Kong: Apa Production, 1974.

Irwin, G. *Nineteenth Century Borneo*. Singapore: Donald Moore, 1955.

Kawasaki, Ichiro. *Japan Unmasked*. Tokyo: Tuttle, 1972.

Klausner, W.J. *Reflections in a Log Pond*. Bangkok: Suksit Siam, 1974.

Legge, J.D. *Indonesia*. New Jersey: Prentice Hall, 1964.

Majul, C.A. *Muslims in the Philippines*. Quezon City: University of the Philippines Press, 1973.

Marcos, Ferdinand E. *The Democratic Revolution in the Philippines*. New Jersey: Prentice Hall, 1974.

Mason, R.H.P. and Caiger, J.G. *A History of Japan*. Melbourne: Cassell, 1972.

Mercado, L.N. *Elements of Filipino Philosophy*. Tacloban City: Divine Word University, 1974.

Mole, R.L. *Thai Values and Behaviour Patterns*. Tokyo: Tuttle, 1973.

Moore, C.E., ed. *The Japanese Mind*. Tokyo: Tuttle, 1973.

Nakane, Chie. *Japanese Society*. Harmondsworth, Penguin, 1973.

Okudaira, Hideo. *Arts of Japan 5: Narrative Picture Scrolls*. New York: Weatherill, and Tokyo: Shibundo, 1973.

Ongkili, J.P. *Modernization in East Malaysia 1960–1970*. Kuala Lumpur: Oxford University Press, 1972.

Polomka, P. *Indonesia Since Sukarno*. Ringwood: Penguin, 1971.

Rawson, P. *The Art of Southeast Asia*. London: Thames and Hudson, 1967.

Roff, W.R. *The Origins of Malay Nationalism*. Kuala Lumpur: University of Malaya Press, 1974.

Ryan, N.J. *The Cultural Heritage of Malaya*. Kuala Lumpur, Longman, 1972.

Scott, W.H. *The Discovery of the Igorots*. Quezon City: New Day, 1974.

———. *On the Cordillera*. Manila: M.C.S. Enterprises, 1969.

———. *The Igorot Struggle for Independence* (monograph). Quezon City: Malaya Books, 1972.

Sheppard, Tan Sri Dato Mubin. *Taman Indera*. Kuala Lumpur: Oxford University Press, 1972.

———. ed. *Singapore 150 Years*. Singapore: Malaysian Branch Royal Asiatic Society Reprint No. 1, 1973.

Stover, L.E. *The Cultural Ecology of Chinese Civilization*. New York: New American Library, 1974.

Suzuki, D.T. *Shin Buddhism*. London: George Allen and Unwin, 1970.

Tazawa, Yutaka, et. al. *Japan's Cultural History: A Perspective*. Tokyo: Ministry of Foreign Affairs, 1973.

Tenazas, Rosa C.P. *The Santo Nino of Cebu*. Cebu City: San Carlos University, 1965.

Tregonning, K.G. *A History of Modern Malaysia and Singapore*. Singapore: Eastern Universities Press, 1972.

Varley, H.P. *Japanese Culture: A Short History*. Tokyo: Tuttle, 1974.

Wang Gungwu, ed. *Malaysia—A Survey*. London: Pall Mall Press, 1964.

Williams, G. *Guide to Yogyakarta*. Yogyakarta: Kanisius, 1974.

Winstedt, R.O. *A History of Malaya*. Kuala Lumpur: Marican, 1968.

Index

thailand

malay

singapore

in